EASY ELEGANT DINING

A COLLECTION OF ELEGANT RECIPES ESPECIALLY CREATED FOR THE PHYSICALLY CHALLENGED AND VISUALLY IMPAIRED AND FOR ANYONE WHO WISHES TO MAKE MEMORABLE DINNERS WITH EASE

by

GRATIA GREENE ALKIRE

ILLUSTRATED BY MICHAEL CADIEUX

TIA PUBLISHING, EMMAUS, PENNSYLVANIA

© 1993, TIA PUBLISHING
P. O. BOX 567, EMMAUS, PA 18049-0567
ALL RIGHTS RESERVED
ISBN 0-9630492-0-8
LIBRARY OF CONGRESS NUMBER 91-075236
EDITED BY PAULA J. BRISCO
DESIGNED AND TYPESET BY SMS TYPOGRAPHY
PRINTED IN THE UNITED STATES OF AMERICA

ACKNOWLEDGMENTS

THANKS TO ALL MY FAMILY AND FRIENDS WHO, THROUGH THE PAST FORTY YEARS, HAVE CONTRIBUTED RECIPES AND SUGGESTIONS. NOT TO BE OVERLOOKED ARE THE TASTE-TESTERS AND REVIEWERS. THEIR INPUT WAS INVALUABLE! THANKS ALSO GOES TO MY HUSBAND, ED, MY SON, TI, AND MY MOTHER-IN-LAW, MARGIE, FOR THEIR HELP AND SUPPORT. I WOULD LIKE TO ACKNOWLEDGE EDIE STAHLNECKER FOR HER CHEERFUL, UNTIRING ASSISTANCE IN ORGANIZING THIS MANUSCRIPT. SPECIAL RECOGNITION GOES TO BEVERLY D. ROMAN, WHO ENCOURAGED ME TO WRITE THIS BOOK IN THE FIRST PLACE AND GUIDED ME THROUGH THE INTRICACIES OF SELF-PUBLISHING.

EASY ELEGANT DINING
IS DEDICATED TO THOSE WHO
ARE MEETING THE CHALLENGES OF
PHYSICAL DISABILITIES OR VISUAL IMPAIRMENTS.

ABOUT THE AUTHOR

 INSPIRED BY HER MOTHER'S LOVE OF COOKING, GRATIA GREENE ALKIRE HAS FOR OVER 40 YEARS COLLECTED AND CREATED RECIPES THAT HAVE DELIGHTED HER FAMILY AND FRIENDS. HER BUSY SCHEDULE (WHICH HAS INCLUDED THE ROLES OF ENGINEER AND MATHEMATICIAN, WIFE, MOTHER, CIVIC VOLUNTEER, AND STOCK ANALYST) ALWAYS MADE IT IMPERATIVE THAT SHE BALANCE CONVENIENCE WITH ELEGANCE IN HER CULINARY CREATIONS.

NOW EVEN WITH IMPAIRED VISION AND SOME PHYSICAL CURTAILMENT DUE TO MULTIPLE SCLEROSIS, SHE HAS NOT FOUND IT NECESSARY TO SIGNIFICANTLY ALTER HER COOKING LIFE-STYLE. INSTEAD, THESE CHANGES IN HER LIFE LED GRATIA TO WRITE *EASY ELEGANT DINING*. SHE HAS REWRITTEN MANY OF HER FAVORITE RECIPES TO SHARE WITH COOKS WHO ARE EQUALLY CHALLENGED.

ABOUT THE ILLUSTRATOR

A GRADUATE OF THE UNIVERSITY OF FLORIDA, MICHAEL J. CADIEUX IS A GRAPHIC DESIGNER. MICHAEL IS PRESENTLY EMPLOYED BY AN INTERNATIONAL PUBLISHING COMPANY IN FT. LAUDERDALE, WHERE HE USES ELECTRONICS TO CREATE UNIQUE DESIGNS. MICHAEL HAS RECEIVED NATIONAL AWARDS FOR HIS WORK. *EASY ELEGANT DINING* IS THE THIRD BOOK HE HAS ILLUSTRATED.

CONTENTS

PREFACE

HAVE PHYSICAL DISABILITIES, VISUAL IMPAIRMENTS, OR OTHER PROBLEMS PREVENTED YOU FROM COOKING THE WAY YOU USED TO? YOUR CULINARY LIFE-STYLE DOESN'T HAVE TO CHANGE RADICALLY. *EASY ELEGANT DINING* COULD BE YOUR KEY TO INDEPENDENCE IN THE KITCHEN!

EASY ELEGANT DINING WAS ESPECIALLY CREATED FOR THE PHYSICALLY DISABLED AND VISUALLY IMPAIRED. ALL OF THE 130+ RECIPES IN THIS BOOK HAVE BEEN TESTED BY THE AUTHOR (WHO IS DISABLED AND VISUALLY IMPAIRED) AND THE RECIPES CAN EASILY BE PREPARED WITH THE AID OF BLENDERS, FOOD PROCESSORS, MICROWAVE OVENS, MIXERS, AND COMMON KITCHEN GADGETS. THE RECIPES HAVE ALSO BEEN REVIEWED AND TESTED BY OTHER DISABLED PEOPLE, AND BY DOCTORS AND OCCUPATIONAL THERAPISTS WHO ARE EXPERTS IN THIS AREA. NOT ALL PEOPLE HAVE THE SAME LIMITATIONS. OUR GOAL HAS BEEN TO PROVIDE RECIPES THAT CAN BE DONE BY MOST PEOPLE.

THE LARGE-PRINT FORMAT IS SPECIFICALLY DESIGNED FOR PEOPLE WITH IMPAIRED VISION. THOSE WITH NORMAL VISION, HOWEVER, WILL ALSO FIND THIS COOKBOOK HELPFUL, AS IT IS EXTREMELY EASY TO READ AND MAY ELIMINATE THE NEED FOR WEARING THOSE ANNOYING READING GLASSES DURING FOOD PREPARATION.

USE *EASY ELEGANT DINING* TO DO EVERYDAY COOKING FOR YOU AND YOUR FAMILY. THIS BOOK WILL ALSO HELP YOU BREEZE RIGHT THROUGH A SPECTACULAR DINNER PARTY. YOU ARE SURE TO BOW TO BRAVOS AND HEAR CRIES OF "ENCORE! ENCORE!"

RECIPE CODES FOR THE
EASY ELEGANT DINING COOKBOOK

[B]   BLENDER

[F]   FOOD PROCESSOR

[L]   LOW FAT

[L+]   POSSIBLE LOW FAT*

[M]   MICROWAVE

[X]   MIXER

*ALL THE RECIPES IN *EASY ELEGANT DINING* HAVE BEEN TESTED WITH ORDINARY EVERYDAY INGREDIENTS. HOWEVER, IF ONE DESIRES LOW FAT OR REDUCED CHOLESTEROL RECIPES, SUBSTITUTION OF LOW FAT PRODUCTS MIGHT PRODUCE SUCCESSFUL RESULTS. THERE ARE MANY LOW FAT FOODS AVAILABLE IN MOST SUPERMARKETS. CONSIDER REDUCED FAT MAYONNAISE, SOUR CREAM, CHEESE, EGGS, AND EVEN LOW FAT BUTTER, JUST TO NAME A FEW. ALTHOUGH LOW FAT BUTTER IS NOT RECOMMENDED FOR BAKING, IT CAN BE USED FOR SAUTÉING VEGETABLES OR LIGHT BROWNING OF MEATS AND POULTRY.

APPETIZERS
BEVERAGES

APPETIZERS • BEVERAGES

EASY MUSHROOM-LIVER PÂTÉ [F]

1/4 CUP BUTTER

1/2 POUND MUSHROOMS

1/2 TEASPOON SALT

1/2 TEASPOON FRESHLY GROUND PEPPER

1/2 POUND LIVERWURST

8-OUNCE PACKAGE CREAM CHEESE

1 TABLESPOON COGNAC (OPTIONAL)

1. ALLOW LIVERWURST AND CREAM CHEESE TO REACH ROOM TEMPERATURE. CHOP MUSHROOMS.

2. MELT BUTTER OVER MEDIUM HEAT. ADD MUSHROOMS, SALT, PEPPER, AND SAUTÉ UNTIL MUSHROOMS ARE SOFTENED AND LIQUID HAS EVAPORATED.

3. COMBINE MUSHROOMS WITH LIVERWURST AND CREAM CHEESE IN BOWL OF FOOD PROCESSOR. MIX THOROUGHLY. ADD OPTIONAL COGNAC.

4. PACK INTO CROCK OR MOLD LINED WITH PLASTIC WRAP. COVER AND REFRIGERATE OVERNIGHT TO ALLOW FLAVORS TO BLEND. SERVE ON CRACKERS OR **TOAST CRISPS**. THIS PÂTÉ CAN BE FROZEN FOR UP TO 2 MONTHS.

YIELD: ABOUT 2 CUPS

TWO-BIT TIDBITS [F]

1/2 POUND SHARP CHEDDAR CHEESE
1 CUP FLOUR   1/2 CUP BUTTER
1/2 ENVELOPE DRY ONION SOUP MIX

1. HEAT OVEN TO 350°F. SHRED CHEDDAR CHEESE. BLEND THOROUGHLY WITH THE 3 REMAINING INGREDIENTS.

2. FORM INTO A ROLL 1 INCH IN DIAMETER. WRAP IN ALUMINUM FOIL AND REFRIGERATE AT LEAST 1 HOUR OR UNTIL NEEDED. THE DOUGH CAN BE FROZEN FOR UP TO 2 MONTHS.

3. WHEN READY TO BAKE, CUT INTO 1/4-INCH THICK SLICES AND PLACE ON COOKIE SHEET. BAKE FOR 6 TO 8 MINUTES. STORE IN AN AIRTIGHT CONTAINER.

YIELD: ABOUT 3 DOZEN

CHICKEN BREAST RUMAKI

1/4 CUP EACH OF SOY SAUCE AND SHERRY
3 BONELESS, SKINLESS CHICKEN BREASTS*
1 CAN SLICED WATER CHESTNUTS
1/2 POUND BACON

1. COMBINE SOY SAUCE AND SHERRY.

2. SLICE EACH CHICKEN BREAST INTO 12 PIECES. MARINATE CHICKEN PIECES IN THE SOY SAUCE/SHERRY MIXTURE AT LEAST 1 HOUR IN THE REFRIGERATOR. DRAIN.

3. PREHEAT BROILER. WRAP WATER CHESTNUT AND A PIECE OF CHICKEN IN 1/2 SLICE BACON. FASTEN WITH TOOTHPICKS. BROIL, TURNING FREQUENTLY, ABOUT 6 TO 7 MINUTES, OR UNTIL BACON IS CRISP AND COOKED THOROUGHLY. SERVE WARM.

*SCALLOPS MAY BE SUBSTITUTED FOR CHICKEN.
PROCEED WITH ABOVE DIRECTIONS.

YIELD: 36 KABOBS

THESE MORSELS CAN BE THREADED ON A LONG SKEWER AND COOKED ON AN OUTDOOR GRILL UNTIL BACON IS CRISP. SERVE WITH RICE, FRESH PINEAPPLE SPEARS, AND A VEGGIE OF YOUR CHOICE.

YIELD: 3 TO 4 SERVINGS

SHRIMP COCKTAIL PÂTÉ [F]

8-OUNCE PACKAGE CREAM CHEESE
2 7-OUNCE CANS SHRIMP*

1/2 SMALL CHOPPED ONION
1 TEASPOON DRY MUSTARD

DASH SALT

1. SLIGHTLY SOFTEN CREAM CHEESE. RINSE AND DRAIN SHRIMP.

2. PROCESS SHRIMP AND ONION IN FOOD PROCESSOR UNTIL FINELY CHOPPED. ADD CREAM CHEESE, DRY MUSTARD, AND SALT. WHIRL UNTIL THOROUGHLY BLENDED.

3. REFRIGERATE COVERED FOR AT LEAST 8 HOURS OR OVERNIGHT.

4. PLACE ON SERVING PLATE. FORM INTO A SMOOTH MOUND AND COVER WITH HOT SAUCE. HOT SAUCE MAY BE PURCHASED OR YOU CAN MAKE YOUR OWN BY COMBINING HORSERADISH AND KETCHUP TO TASTE. SERVE WITH CRACKERS OR **TOAST CRISPS**. MAKE ADDITIONAL HOT SAUCE AVAILABLE.

YIELD: ABOUT 10 OUNCES SHRIMP PÂTÉ

*2 7-OUNCE CANS OF SHRIMP MAKE 9 OUNCES OF DRY WEIGHT SHRIMP, WHICH IS WHAT IS NEEDED FOR THIS RECIPE.

CRABBY MUSHROOMS

24 MEDIUM MUSHROOMS, STEMS REMOVED

4 FRESH OR FROZEN CRAB PATTIES   2 TABLESPOONS FRESH PARSLEY

8 CHOPPED, RIPE OLIVES   GRATED PARMESAN CHEESE

1. SET OVEN TO 350°F.

2. WASH AND DRY MUSHROOM CAPS.

3. IN A BOWL, BLEND THAWED CRAB PATTIES WITH SNIPPED PARSLEY AND OLIVES. FILL MUSHROOM CAPS WITH MIXTURE.

4. RINSE BAKING SHEET LIGHTLY WITH WATER, SHAKING OFF EXCESS. ARRANGE MUSHROOMS ON SHEET. COVER WITH TENT OF FOIL AND BAKE 12 TO 15 MINUTES. REMOVE FOIL, SPRINKLE WITH CHEESE, AND BROIL UNTIL CHEESE IS MELTED AND MUSHROOMS ARE GOLDEN, ABOUT 2 MINUTES. SERVE IMMEDIATELY.

YIELD: 24 STUFFED MUSHROOMS

THIS IS AN EASY WAY TO STUFF MUSHROOMS WITH CRABMEAT.

HOT SPICY WINE PUNCH

3/4 CUP BROWN SUGAR, FIRMLY PACKED

2 TEASPOONS GROUND CINNAMON   1 TEASPOON GROUND CLOVES

1/2 TEASPOON EACH GRATED LEMON AND ORANGE PEELS

1 TEASPOON GROUND ALLSPICE   1/2 TEASPOON GROUND NUTMEG

1. COMBINE ALL INGREDIENTS. STORE MIX IN AN AIRTIGHT CONTAINER UNTIL READY TO USE.

YIELD: 3/4 CUP DRY MIX

2. FOR 2 SERVINGS OF WINE PUNCH, COMBINE 1/4 CUP MIX WITH 1 CUP RED WINE AND 1/4 CUP WATER. BRING TO A BOIL OVER MEDIUM HEAT. REDUCE HEAT AND SIMMER 5 MINUTES.

SPICED DEMITASSE

1 CUP REGULAR GRIND COFFEE

6 SUGAR CUBES   5 WHOLE CLOVES

8 WHOLE ALLSPICE   8 INCHES OF CINNAMON STICK

FILL COFFEEPOT WITH 6 CUPS COLD WATER. PUT ALL INGREDIENTS INTO COFFEE BASKET. PERC AS USUAL.

YIELD: 10 TO 12 DEMITASSE CUPS

PICTURE THIS. IT'S WINTER. YOU'VE JUST FINISHED A DELICIOUS DINNER. YOU AND YOUR GUESTS RELAX IN FRONT OF A ROARING FIRE SIPPING DEMITASSE. EVEN WITHOUT SNOW IT'S PERFECT!

SUMMERTIME PUNCH

2 QUARTS CRANBERRY JUICE

1 QUART CRANBERRY-APPLE JUICE

6-OUNCE CAN FROZEN LEMONADE

2 QUARTS GINGER ALE

LEMON SLICES

1. MIX ALL INGREDIENTS TOGETHER, RESERVING 1 QUART CRANBERRY JUICE. CHILL.

2. MAKE ICE CUBES WITH REMAINING CRANBERRY JUICE.

3. PUT PUNCH AND ICE CUBES IN PUNCH BOWL. FLOAT LEMON SLICES ON TOP.

YIELD: 32 4-OUNCE SERVINGS

THIS IS A GREAT NON-ALCOHOLIC PUNCH TO SERVE WITH PASTRIES FOR AFTERNOON TEA. TO MAKE THIS ALCOHOLIC, JUST ADD 1 CUP OF VODKA.

WINTER WARM-UP

1 PINT TOMATO OR VEGETABLE JUICE
1 PINT STRONG BEEF BOUILLON
1 SMALL ONION, STUCK WITH 4 CLOVES

1 LEMON, CUT INTO WEDGES
FRESHLY GROUND PEPPER
VODKA (OPTIONAL)

1. IN PAN, COMBINE TOMATO OR VEGETABLE JUICE, BEEF BOUILLON, AND CLOVE-STUDDED ONION. BRING ALL TO BOIL. REDUCE HEAT AND SIMMER 5 MINUTES.

2. REMOVE ONION. SERVE IN MUGS WITH LEMON WEDGES, PEPPER, AND VODKA, IF DESIRED.

YIELD: 4 TO 6 SERVINGS

THIS WOULD WARM YOU UP AFTER YOUR FAVORITE WINTER OUTDOOR ACTIVITY.

EGGS CHEESE SAUCES

EGGS • CHEESE • SAUCES

HINTS:

AN EGG SEPARATOR MAKES SEPARATING THE YOLK FROM THE WHITE EASY. THE DEVICE OFTEN CAN FASTEN OVER A CUP, MAKING IT ALMOST A ONE-HANDED OPERATION.

SOMETIMES A RECIPE REQUIRES SLIGHTLY BEATEN EGGS. WE USE AN EGG BEATER WHICH RESEMBLES A SPRING ON A WOODEN HANDLE THAT IS PUMPED UP AND DOWN WITH ONE HAND. THESE MIGHT BE HARD TO COME BY, BUT IF YOU FIND ONE, BUY IT.

YOU DON'T HAVE TO WIND SPAGHETTI TO GET A FORKFUL. USE ROTINI AND ROTELLI IN YOUR PASTA DISHES. THEY ABSORB SAUCES BETTER AND ARE EASIER TO EAT. SEE **PASTA WITH WHITE CLAM SAUCE** IN THE **FISH AND SHELLFISH** SECTION.

INCREDIBLE PANCAKE

1/2 CUP FLOUR

1/2 CUP MILK

2 EGGS, LIGHTLY BEATEN

PINCH NUTMEG

1/4 CUP BUTTER

JUICE OF 1/2 LEMON

2 TABLESPOONS CONFECTIONERS' SUGAR

1. SET OVEN TO 425°F. COMBINE FLOUR, MILK, EGGS, AND NUTMEG. **BATTER WILL BE A LITTLE LUMPY; DO NOT BEAT.**

2. MELT BUTTER IN A 10-INCH, OVENPROOF SKILLET. POUR IN BATTER WHEN SKILLET IS VERY HOT BUT BUTTER IS NOT BURNED.

3. BAKE IN OVEN FOR 15 TO 20 MINUTES. SPRINKLE WITH CONFECTIONERS' SUGAR AND LEMON JUICE. RETURN TO OVEN FOR 2 MINUTES.

4. SERVE WITH JAM OR MORE LEMON JUICE AND SUGAR.

YIELD: 2 SERVINGS

MAMMA MIA, THAT'S A QUICHE! [F]

1 UNBAKED PIE SHELL

3 EGGS, BEATEN

1 CUP MILK

1/2 TEASPOON OREGANO

3/4 CUP EACH GRATED MOZZARELLA AND SWISS CHEESE

1/2 CUP EACH COARSELY CHOPPED PEPPERONI AND GREEN PEPPER

1. BAKE UNBAKED PIE SHELL AT 375°F FOR 5 MINUTES TO SET. TURN OVEN DOWN TO 325°F.

2. MIX REMAINING INGREDIENTS TOGETHER, POUR INTO PREPARED SHELL, OR REFRIGERATE FILLING UNTIL READY TO BAKE.

3. BAKE FOR 1 HOUR.

YIELD: 6 SERVINGS

FOR A RELAXING FRIDAY NIGHT SUPPER, A QUICHE, SALAD, CRUSTY BREAD, AND MAYBE SOME FRUIT WOULD BE A LAID-BACK WAY TO END A VERY BUSY WEEK.

CHEESE LOVER'S MACARONI AND... [M]

2 CUPS ELBOW MACARONI

3 TABLESPOONS BUTTER

3 TABLESPOONS FLOUR

2 1/2 CUPS MILK

SALT AND WHITE OR BLACK PEPPER (OPTIONAL)

2 1/2 CUPS SHREDDED SHARP CHEDDAR CHEESE

1/2 CUP SHREDDED MOZZARELLA CHEESE

1/4 CUP FRESHLY GRATED PARMESAN CHEESE

PAPRIKA

1. COOK MACARONI ACCORDING TO PACKAGE DIRECTIONS. DRAIN.

2. MELT BUTTER IN MICROWAVE AND BLEND IN FLOUR. ADD MILK, RETURN TO MICROWAVE, AND STIR EVERY 30 SECONDS UNTIL THICKENED.

3. ADD SEASONINGS AND CHEDDAR AND MOZZARELLA CHEESES, STIRRING UNTIL CHEESE IS MELTED.

4. COMBINE SAUCE WITH COOKED MACARONI AND MIX WELL. TURN INTO A GREASED 9 X 13-INCH CASSEROLE.

5. SPRINKLE WITH PARMESAN CHEESE AND PAPRIKA. BAKE AT 350°F FOR 40 MINUTES.

YIELD: 8 TO 10 SERVINGS

SAUTÉED CHOPPED ONION AND GREEN PEPPER COULD BE ADDED TO THIS RECIPE FOR COLOR AND A DIFFERENT FLAVOR. TOMATOES GO WELL WITH CHEESE, SO TRY A TOSSED SALAD OF TOMATOES, CUCUMBERS, AND ONIONS TO ACCOMPANY THIS DISH.

VEGETARIAN PIZZA [M]

---

1 TUBE (10 OUNCES) REFRIGERATED PIZZA DOUGH
10 OUNCES FROZEN, CHOPPED SPINACH

2 CUPS SHREDDED MOZZARELLA CHEESE

8 BLACK OLIVES

1 CLOVE GARLIC, MINCED

1/2 MEDIUM ONION

3/4 CUP PIZZA SAUCE

1/4 CUP PARMESAN CHEESE

1. PREHEAT OVEN TO 425°F. LIGHTLY OIL (OLIVE OIL WOULD BE PERFECT) AN 8- OR 9-INCH SQUARE BAKING PAN. PAT DOUGH IN BOTTOM AND UP SIDES, FITTING CLOSELY WHERE BOTTOM AND SIDES MEET. TRIM OFF EXCESS DOUGH BY RUNNING A SHARP KNIFE AROUND EDGE.

2. THAW SPINACH BY REMOVING FROM PACKAGE, PLACING IN A MICROWAVE-SAFE BOWL. MICROWAVE ON HIGH POWER FOR 2 TO 3 MINUTES. PLACE SPINACH IN A SIEVE AND PRESS OUT ALL MOISTURE WITH THE BACK OF A LARGE SPOON.

3. COMBINE SPINACH WITH MOZZARELLA CHEESE AND GARLIC. MIX THOROUGHLY WITH HANDS TO BREAK UP CLUMPS OF SPINACH. LAYER OVER DOUGH. SPREAD SAUCE OVER CHEESE/SPINACH MIXTURE.

4. BAKE FOR 10 MINUTES. MEANWHILE, THINLY SLICE OLIVES AND ONION. AFTER REMOVING PIZZA FROM OVEN, ARRANGE OLIVES AND ONIONS ON TOP OF PIZZA. TOP WITH PARMESAN CHEESE AND BAKE FOR 10 ADDITIONAL MINUTES. LET STAND ABOUT 5 MINUTES BEFORE CUTTING.

YIELD: 4 SERVINGS

VERSATILE SOUFFLÉ [X]

1/2 POUND CRABMEAT*

8 SLICES BREAD, CRUSTS REMOVED

2 TABLESPOONS MINCED ONION

2 TABLESPOONS MINCED PARSLEY

4 EGGS

2 CUPS MILK

1/2 TEASPOON DRY MUSTARD

1/8 TEASPOON PEPPER

1 1/4 CUPS SHREDDED CHEDDAR CHEESE

1. RINSE, DRAIN, AND SLICE CRABMEAT. BUTTER AND CUBE BREAD.

2. PLACE HALF THE BREAD CUBES IN AN 8-INCH-SQUARE BUTTERED BAKING DISH. SPRINKLE WITH ONION AND PARSLEY. SPREAD SLICED CRAB OVER VEGETABLES. SPRINKLE WITH 1 CUP OF CHEESE. TOP WITH REMAINING BREAD CUBES.

3. BEAT EGGS WITH MILK AND SEASONINGS. POUR OVER INGREDIENTS IN CASSEROLE. REFRIGERATE COVERED AT LEAST 8 HOURS OR OVERNIGHT.

4. BAKE AT 325°F FOR 1 HOUR, SPRINKLING WITH REMAINING 1/4 CUP SHREDDED CHEESE PRIOR TO THE LAST 15 MINUTES OF BAKING. LET STAND 5 TO 10 MINUTES BEFORE CUTTING INTO SQUARES TO SERVE.

YIELD: 4 TO 6 SERVINGS

1/2 POUND DRIED BEEF CUT INTO SLIVERS, FRIED BULK SAUSAGE, OR COOKED CRUMBLED BACON CAN BE SUBSTITUTED FOR THE CRAB. WITH BACON OR SAUSAGE, THIS IS A MARVELOUS DO-AHEAD BREAKFAST. A SALAD AND THIS SOUFFLÉ, MADE WITH CRABMEAT OR DRIED BEEF, MAKES AN EASY, ELEGANT LUNCH.

GREEN FETTUCCINE WITH CHEESE AND MUSHROOMS

1/3 TO 1/2 POUND GREEN FETTUCCINE

3 TABLESPOONS BUTTER

3/4 CUP SLICED MUSHROOMS

1 CLOVE GARLIC, MINCED

SALT

FRESHLY GROUND PEPPER

1/2 CUP FRESHLY GRATED PARMESAN CHEESE

1. BRING A LARGE POT OF SALTED WATER TO A BOIL AND COOK FETTUCCINE FOLLOWING PACKAGE DIRECTIONS.

2. MELT BUTTER. SAUTÉ MUSHROOMS AND GARLIC UNTIL TENDER BUT STILL FIRM.

3. TO SERVE, DRAIN PASTA THOROUGHLY. RETURN PASTA TO COOKING POT. OVER VERY LOW HEAT, COMBINE SAUTÉED MUSHROOMS AND CHEESE. TOSS GENTLY AND SERVE ON **HEATED** PLATES. MAKE FRESHLY GROUND PEPPER AND ADDITIONAL GRATED PARMESAN CHEESE AVAILABLE.

YIELD: 2 SMALL SERVINGS

GREEN FETTUCCINE WITH CHEESE AND MUSHROOMS IS A GREAT SIDE DISH FOR ANY ITALIAN-STYLE ENTRÉE.

VELVET FUDGE SAUCE [M, B]

14 1/2 OUNCES EVAPORATED MILK
2 CUPS SUGAR
4 OUNCES BAKING CHOCOLATE

1/4 CUP BUTTER
1 TEASPOON VANILLA
1/2 TEASPOON SALT

1. IN MICROWAVE-SAFE DISH, HEAT MILK AND SUGAR. BRING TO A FULL BOIL. CONTINUE HEATING UNTIL SUGAR IS DISSOLVED, STIRRING EVERY MINUTE.

2. ADD CHOCOLATE AND STIR OCCASIONALLY UNTIL MELTED. POUR INTO BLENDER CONTAINER AND BLEND UNTIL SMOOTH.

3. ADD BUTTER, VANILLA, AND SALT. CONTINUE BLENDING UNTIL ALL INGREDIENTS ARE THOROUGHLY MIXED.

YIELD: 3 CUPS

THIS SAUCE WARMED MAKES AN EXTRAORDINARY HOT FUDGE SUNDAE! TOSS ON A HANDFUL OF SPANISH PEANUTS AND VOILA! A MEXICAN SUNDAE IS CREATED.

LEMON SAUCE À LA ELGIN [M]

1 LEMON

GENEROUS 1/4 CUP SUGAR

3/4 CUP WATER

1 TABLESPOON CORNSTARCH

1 TABLESPOON BUTTER

1. CUT LEMON IN HALF AND SQUEEZE 2 TABLESPOONS OF JUICE. PLACE JUICE AND LEMON RINDS IN A 1-QUART MICROWAVE-SAFE DISH. ADD SUGAR AND 1/2 CUP OF THE WATER. BRING TO A BOIL, STIRRING EVERY 15 SECONDS UNTIL SUGAR IS DISSOLVED.

2. STIR CORNSTARCH INTO REMAINING 1/4 CUP WATER. ADD TO LEMON MIXTURE AND COOK FOR 2 MINUTES ON HIGH HEAT, STIRRING CONSTANTLY IF ON STOVE TOP OR EVERY 30 SECONDS IF IN MICROWAVE. MIXTURE SHOULD BE SLIGHTLY THICKENED AND CLEAR.

3. REMOVE LEMON RINDS, SQUEEZING THE RINDS FOR EXTRA JUICE. ADD EXTRA SUGAR TO TASTE IF NEEDED. PUT IN BUTTER AND STIR UNTIL MELTED. SERVE WARM.

YIELD: ABOUT 3/4 CUP

THIS IS A GREAT TOPPING FOR GINGERBREAD OR ANGEL FOOD CAKE.

RUM SAUCE [M]

1/2 CUP WATER
1/2 CUP SUGAR
1/2 CUP BUTTER
1/2-INCH PIECE VANILLA BEAN

1 SLICE LEMON
1/2 SLICE ORANGE
1 CLOVE
1-INCH STICK CINNAMON

1/2 CUP RUM

1. BRING ALL INGREDIENTS EXCEPT RUM TO A BOIL, STIRRING UNTIL THE SUGAR HAS DISSOLVED. SIMMER 5 MINUTES.

2. STRAIN, LET COOL A BIT, AND ADD THE RUM.

YIELD: APPROXIMATELY 2 CUPS

WHITE AND MORNAY SAUCES [M]

2 TABLESPOONS BUTTER
2 TABLESPOONS FLOUR

1/2 TEASPOON SALT
1 CUP MILK

1/2 TO 1 CUP GRATED CHEDDAR CHEESE (FOR MORNAY SAUCE OPTION)

1. MELT BUTTER IN MICROWAVE-SAFE SAUCEPAN. ADD FLOUR AND SALT AND COOK UNTIL BUBBLY.

2. GRADUALLY ADD MILK. RETURN TO MICROWAVE AND COOK, STIRRING EVERY MINUTE UNTIL THICKENED, ABOUT 3 OR 4 MINUTES.

3. REMOVE ANY LUMPS BY BLENDING IN A BLENDER. FOR MORNAY SAUCE, ADD GRATED CHEESE AND HEAT UNTIL MELTED.

YIELD: 1 TO 1 1/2 CUPS

HORSERADISH–SOUR CREAM AND CHIVE SAUCE

1 CUP DAIRY SOUR CREAM

2 TEASPOONS SUGAR

3 TABLESPOONS FRESH HORSERADISH

1 TABLESPOON CHOPPED CHIVES

COMBINE ALL INGREDIENTS. REFRIGERATE. SERVE ON ROAST OR CORNED BEEF.

YIELD: 1 CUP

ANOTHER WAY TO MAKE A HORSERADISH SAUCE IS TO WHIP 1 CUP OF HEAVY CREAM; OMIT SUGAR AND CHIVES AND JUST ADD 3 TABLESPOONS HORSERADISH. THIS IS DIFFERENT AND VERY GOOD.

STIR-FRY GLAZE [M]

1 TABLESPOON SUGAR

1/2 CUP COLD WATER

2 TABLESPOONS CORNSTARCH

1/4 CUP SOY SAUCE

2 TABLESPOONS DRY SHERRY

COMBINE ALL INGREDIENTS IN A MICROWAVE-SAFE DISH. BLEND WELL TO DISSOLVE SUGAR AND CORNSTARCH. BRING TO A BOIL. WHEN THICK AND SHINY, REMOVE FROM MICROWAVE.

YIELD: 1 CUP

THIS GLAZE PERKS UP STIR-FRIED VEGGIES, BEEF, CHICKEN, OR SHRIMP. ADDING A TEASPOON OF CHOPPED, FRESH GINGER OR CRYSTALLIZED GINGER GIVES ORIENTAL FOOD THAT AUTHENTIC TOUCH.

SOUPS
SALADS
DRESSINGS

SOUPS • SALADS • DRESSINGS

HINTS:

TO MAKE YOUR SALAD MEMORABLE, SERVE IT ON A COLD PLATE. PREPARE YOUR GREENS BY WASHING THEM, ROLLING THEM UP IN A BATH TOWEL, AND RUNNING THEM IN THE SPIN-DRY CYCLE OF YOUR **TOP-LOADING** WASHING MACHINE. CRISP IN REFRIGERATOR.

WE RECOMMEND USING FRESHLY GROUND PEPPER, FRESH GARLIC, AND FRESH PARSLEY IN RECIPES. FRESH IS FAR SUPERIOR!

CRAB BISQUE [F]

2 TABLESPOONS ONION
3 TABLESPOONS BUTTER
3 TABLESPOONS FLOUR
3 CUPS MILK
2 CHICKEN BOUILLON CUBES

DASH OF PAPRIKA
1 CUP LIGHT CREAM
1 CUP FRESH CRABMEAT
2 TABLESPOONS CHOPPED CHIVES
3 TO 5 TABLESPOONS DRY SHERRY

1. FINELY CHOP ONION. IN A LARGE SAUCEPAN, SAUTÉ ONION IN BUTTER UNTIL SOFT. ADD FLOUR. MIX WELL FOR ABOUT A MINUTE.

2. SLOWLY ADD MILK, BOUILLON CUBES, PAPRIKA, AND CREAM. COOK OVER LOW HEAT, STIRRING CONSTANTLY, UNTIL THICKENED. **DO NOT BOIL.**

3. TRANSFER TO FOOD PROCESSOR BOWL. ADD 1/2 CUP CRABMEAT AND PROCESS UNTIL **VERY SMOOTH.**

4. CHOP REMAINING CRABMEAT. RETURN PURÉED MIXTURE TO SAUCEPAN AND ADD CRABMEAT, CHIVES, AND SHERRY. IF NECESSARY, ADD ADDITIONAL MILK AND ADJUST SEASONINGS. REHEAT JUST BEFORE SERVING.

YIELD: 6 SERVINGS

FRENCH ONION SOUP

4 LARGE ONIONS, SLICED INTO RINGS

4 TABLESPOONS BUTTER	7 OR 8 BEEF BOUILLON CUBES
1/2 TEASPOON SALT	1 TABLESPOON FLOUR
1/2 TEASPOON SUGAR	1/2 CUP WHITE WINE
6 CUPS WATER	FRENCH BREAD

4 OUNCES SWISS CHEESE, GRATED

1. HEAT BUTTER IN A LARGE SAUCEPAN. ADD ONIONS, COVER, AND SIMMER FOR 15 MINUTES.

2. ADD SALT AND SUGAR. RAISE HEAT SLIGHTLY AND COOK UNCOVERED FOR ANOTHER 20 TO 25 MINUTES OR UNTIL ONIONS TURN GOLDEN BROWN. MEANWHILE, IN A SECOND POT, BRING WATER TO A BOIL, ADD BOUILLON CUBES, AND STIR UNTIL DISSOLVED.

3. ADD FLOUR TO SAUCEPAN AND STIR WITH ONIONS AND BUTTER. COOK FOR 1 MINUTE. SLOWLY ADD BEEF BOUILLON AND WINE. BRING TO A BOIL AND SIMMER SOUP FOR 20 MINUTES, STIRRING FROM TIME TO TIME. TASTE FOR SEASONING.

4. SERVE THE SOUP IN INDIVIDUAL CUPS. FLOAT A TOASTED ROUND OF FRENCH BREAD TOPPED WITH GRATED SWISS CHEESE AND BROIL JUST UNTIL THE CHEESE IS BROWN AND BUBBLY.

YIELD: 4 SERVINGS

CHILLED AVOCADO SOUP [F]

3 FULLY RIPE AVOCADOS
1 CUP CHICKEN BOUILLON
1/4 CUP CHOPPED ONIONS
1 CUP LIGHT CREAM

1 TEASPOON SALT
PINCH OF WHITE PEPPER
1 TEASPOON LEMON JUICE
LEMON SLICES AS GARNISH

1. HALVE AVOCADOS LENGTHWISE AND REMOVE SEEDS AND PEEL.

2. BLEND AVOCADOS, CHICKEN BOUILLON, AND ONIONS IN FOOD PROCESSOR FOR A FEW SECONDS OR UNTIL SMOOTH.

3. ADD CREAM AND SEASONINGS. PROCESS FOR 2 SECONDS TO COMBINE. ADJUST SEASONINGS TO TASTE, IF NECESSARY.

4. POUR INTO CONTAINER. COVER AND REFRIGERATE FOR AT LEAST 3 HOURS OR OVERNIGHT, IF DESIRED. STIR IN LEMON JUICE.

5. SERVE CHILLED IN CHILLED BOWLS, GARNISHED WITH A LEMON SLICE.

YIELD: 4 SERVINGS

CHILLED AVOCADO SOUP IS A REFRESHING CHANGE ON THOSE WARM SPRING OR SUMMER DAYS.

ADZUKI BEAN SOUP

2 CUPS CARROTS, SLICED
4 STALKS CELERY, CHOPPED
1 LARGE ONION, CHOPPED
1 CLOVE GARLIC, MINCED

24-OUNCE JAR ADZUKI BEANS
3 CUPS WATER
1/4 CUP TAMARI SAUCE
1/3 CUP FRESH PARSLEY

SALT, PEPPER, AND ADDITIONAL TAMARI SAUCE TO TASTE

1. SAUTÉ CARROTS, CELERY, ONION, AND GARLIC IN SMALL AMOUNT OF OLIVE OR OTHER OIL, UNTIL ONIONS ARE SLIGHTLY BROWN.

2. ADD BEANS, WATER, AND TAMARI SAUCE. SIMMER FOR 25 MINUTES. STIR OCCASIONALLY.

3. ADJUST SEASONINGS TO TASTE. ADD PARSLEY AND SIMMER FOR A FEW ADDITIONAL MINUTES.

YIELD: 4 GENEROUS SERVINGS

THIS IS A VERY EASY 1-POT SOUP. JUST SAUTÉ THE VEGGIES AND GARLIC, ADD OTHER INGREDIENTS, AND SIMMER. HOW EASY CAN IT BE TO PREPARE A HEALTHY, NUTRITIOUS SOUP?

CURRIED CHICKEN SALAD [L]

3 CUPS COOKED, CUBED CHICKEN

1/2 CUP GREEN GRAPES

1/2 CUP CHOPPED CELERY

1/2 CUP CHOPPED APPLES

1/4 CUP CHOPPED ONION

1/2 CUP COARSELY CHOPPED PECANS

1. COMBINE ALL INGREDIENTS IN A LARGE BOWL.

2. TOSS WITH **CREAMY CURRY-GARLIC DRESSING** (SEE BELOW). REFRIGERATE UNTIL SERVING TIME.

YIELD: 4 SERVINGS

CREAMY CURRY-GARLIC DRESSING [F OR X, L+]

1 CUP MAYONNAISE

1 MASHED CLOVE GARLIC

1/4 TEASPOON GINGER

1 TEASPOON HONEY

1/2 TO 1 TEASPOON CURRY POWDER

1 TABLESPOON LIME JUICE

COMBINE ALL INGREDIENTS.

YIELD: 1 CUP+

THIS WOULD MAKE A NICE WARM-WEATHER LUNCHEON SERVED WITH CRESCENT ROLLS AND ICED TEA, WITH SHERBET AND COOKIES FOR DESSERT.

TOMATO ASPIC SALAD [L]

3-OUNCE PACKAGE LEMON GELATIN
1 CUP MINUS 2 TABLESPOONS BOILING WATER
2 TABLESPOONS VINEGAR OR LEMON JUICE
8-OUNCE CAN TOMATO SAUCE

1. MIX LEMON GELATIN WITH BOILING WATER. STIR UNTIL DISSOLVED.
   ADD VINEGAR OR LEMON JUICE AND CAN OF TOMATO SAUCE.
   STIR AGAIN.

2. POUR IN LIGHTLY GREASED MOLD OF YOUR CHOICE.

3. REFRIGERATE UNTIL SET. UNMOLD ONTO LETTUCE LEAF AND SERVE
   WITH **CUCUMBER-DILL DRESSING** (RECIPE BELOW).

CUCUMBER-DILL DRESSING [L+]

PEELED CUCUMBER, CUT INTO QUARTERS, SEEDS REMOVED,
AND FINELY CHOPPED
1/4 CUP CHOPPED ONION   8 OUNCES SOUR CREAM
1/4 TO 1/2 TEASPOON DILL, TO TASTE
FRESHLY GROUND BLACK PEPPER, TO TASTE

MIX ALL INGREDIENTS. REFRIGERATE UNTIL USED WITH **TOMATO ASPIC
SALAD**. DO NOT PREPARE MORE THAN 12 HOURS BEFORE SERVING AS
DRESSING MAY BECOME WATERY.

YIELD: 4 SERVINGS

TOMATOES VINAIGRETTE [B]

5 MEDIUM TOMATOES

2 CLOVES GARLIC

1/3 CUP WINE VINEGAR

2 TEASPOONS OREGANO

1 TEASPOON SALT

1 CUP OLIVE OIL

1/2 TEASPOON PEPPER

1/2 TEASPOON DRY MUSTARD

1 TABLESPOON MINCED ONION

1 TABLESPOON FINELY CHOPPED PARSLEY

1. WASH TOMATOES AND CUT IN THICK SLICES. ARRANGE IN A PAN OR DISH.

2. FINELY MINCE OR PRESS GARLIC. IN BLENDER, COMBINE WITH ALL OTHER INGREDIENTS EXCEPT ONION AND PARSLEY. PULSE A FEW TIMES TO MIX. IF A BLENDER IS NOT AVAILABLE, PUT IN A CLOSED JAR AND SHAKE VIGOROUSLY. POUR OVER TOMATOES.

3. COVER TOMATOES AND REFRIGERATE FOR 2 OR 3 HOURS, BASTING OCCASIONALLY. TO SERVE, SPRINKLE WITH ONION AND PARSLEY AND SOME OF THE DRESSING.

YIELD: 6 SERVINGS

SALADE COMPOSÉE

1/2 CUP PECANS
14 OUNCES HEARTS OF PALM
11 OUNCES MANDARIN ORANGES
4 OUNCES ARTICHOKE HEARTS
4 CUPS TORN ROMAINE LETTUCE
1/3 CUP OLIVE OIL

3 TEASPOONS VINEGAR
1/2 TEASPOON FRESH CHERVIL*
1/8 TEASPOON THYME
1/4 TEASPOON SUGAR
SALT TO TASTE
PEPPER TO TASTE

1. TOAST PECANS. DRAIN HEARTS OF PALM, MANDARIN ORANGES, AND ARTICHOKE HEARTS.

2. PLACE BITE-SIZED PIECES OF LETTUCE IN A CHILLED SALAD BOWL. CUT HALF OF HEARTS OF PALM INTO 1-INCH SLICES AND REFRIGERATE REMAINDER FOR ANOTHER DAY. COMBINE HEARTS OF PALM WITH MANDARIN ORANGES, ARTICHOKE HEARTS, AND PECANS.

3. COMBINE REMAINING INGREDIENTS AND POUR OVER SALAD. REFRIGERATE COVERED. TOSS LIGHTLY JUST BEFORE SERVING.

YIELD: 6 SERVINGS

*IF FRESH CHERVIL IS NOT AVAILABLE, 1/4 TEASPOON DRIED CHERVIL WILL DO JUST FINE.

INDONESIAN CUCUMBERS

5 CUCUMBERS
2 TABLESPOONS SALT
2 SHALLOTS, MINCED

3 CLOVES GARLIC, MINCED
1 TABLESPOON FRESH GINGER
2 TABLESPOONS PEANUT OIL

2 TABLESPOONS GROUND FINELY CHOPPED ALMONDS (OPTIONAL)

1 1/2 TEASPOONS TURMERIC
1 TABLESPOON SUGAR

1/2 CUP VINEGAR
1/4 CUP WATER

1. PEEL CUCUMBERS AND CUT LENGTHWISE INTO QUARTERS. REMOVE AND DISCARD PULPY CENTERS WITH THE SEEDS. CUT REMAINING QUARTERS INTO BITE-SIZED PIECES AND SALT. PLACE IN REFRIGERATOR FOR 1 HOUR OR MORE.

2. WASH CUCUMBERS IN A BOWL OF COLD WATER AND DRAIN WELL. PRESS THEM IN A CLEAN TOWEL TO REMOVE EXCESS MOISTURE.

3. SAUTÉ SHALLOTS, GARLIC, AND GINGER (CRYSTALLIZED GINGER MAY BE SUBSTITUTED FOR FRESH GINGER) IN PEANUT OIL UNTIL SOFT. ADD ALMONDS, TURMERIC, AND SUGAR. STIR TOGETHER. THEN ADD VINEGAR AND WATER. SIMMER 10 MINUTES.

4. POUR HOT MIXTURE OVER CUCUMBERS. MIX WELL AND LET STAND IN REFRIGERATOR AT LEAST 1 HOUR BEFORE SERVING AS A SIDE DISH FOR CURRIES.

YIELD: 8 TO 10 SERVINGS

ORIENTAL SPINACH SALAD

4 CUPS SPINACH LEAVES   2 TABLESPOONS SOY SAUCE

6 SLICED SCALLIONS   1 TEASPOON WHITE VINEGAR

1 TABLESPOON SALAD OIL

2 TEASPOONS FINELY CHOPPED FRESH OR CRYSTALLIZED GINGER

1/4 POUND MUSHROOMS, THINLY SLICED   3 TABLESPOONS PINE NUTS

1. COMBINE SPINACH LEAVES AND SCALLIONS.

2. MIX SOY SAUCE, WHITE VINEGAR, SALAD OIL, AND GINGER IN COVERED JAR OR CRUET.

3. TOSS DRESSING TOGETHER WITH SPINACH LEAVES, SCALLIONS, AND MUSHROOMS. SPRINKLE WITH PINE NUTS. CHILL AND SERVE.

YIELD: 4 TO 5 SERVINGS

A DIFFERENT CUCUMBER SALAD [B, F]

2 CUPS WHITE VINEGAR

1 CUP WATER

4 TABLESPOONS SOY SAUCE

8 TEASPOONS SUGAR

1/4 CUP GRATED FRESH OR FINELY CHOPPED CRYSTALLIZED GINGER

8 LARGE CUCUMBERS, SLICED THIN

2 LARGE CARROTS, SHREDDED

1 CUP BIAS-SLICED SCALLIONS

1/2 CUP PARSLEY, CHOPPED

1. COMBINE VINEGAR, WATER, SOY SAUCE, SUGAR, AND GINGER IN BLENDER AND WHIRL FOR A FEW SECONDS.

2. PLACE CUCUMBERS, CARROTS, SCALLIONS, AND PARSLEY IN BOWL. POUR CONTENTS OF BLENDER OVER VEGGIES AND TOSS.

3. REFRIGERATE COVERED 2 HOURS OR OVERNIGHT.

4. DRAIN EXCESS LIQUID, ADJUST SEASONINGS, AND SERVE.

YIELD: 6 TO 8 SERVINGS

*DON'T FORGET YOUR FOOD PROCESSOR—IT'S **THE** WAY TO SLICE CUCUMBERS AND GRATE CARROTS.*

TI'S HOMEMADE FRENCH DRESSING [B OR F]

2 CLOVES GARLIC
3/4 CUP OIL
4 TABLESPOONS VINEGAR*
1/4 CUP TOMATO PASTE

2 TABLESPOONS HONEY
1 TEASPOON SALT
1/2 TEASPOON PEPPER
1/2 TEASPOON PAPRIKA

COMBINE ALL INGREDIENTS. PROCESS UNTIL SMOOTH.

YIELD: 1 GENEROUS CUP

TRY USING BALSAMIC VINEGAR IF YOU WANT TO CUT BACK ON THE ACIDITY OF THIS DRESSING.

FLUFFY MUSTARD DRESSING

1 CUP HEAVY CREAM, WHIPPED
1 TABLESPOON HORSERADISH

1/2 CUP MAYONNAISE
2 TABLESPOONS PREPARED MUSTARD

FOLD INGREDIENTS TOGETHER CAREFULLY. SERVE AS A CONDIMENT TO CORNED BEEF. THIS WILL KEEP WELL FOR ABOUT A WEEK IF REFRIGERATED.

YIELD: APPROXIMATELY 2 CUPS

KAY'S DRESSING [B]

2/3 CUP OIL

2 TEASPOONS VINEGAR

1 TEASPOON MUSTARD

3 TEASPOONS SEASONED SALT

1 TABLESPOON SUGAR

3 TABLESPOONS LEMON JUICE

1 TABLESPOON MAYONNAISE

1 CLOVE GARLIC

COMBINE ALL INGREDIENTS IN BLENDER. CHILL.

YIELD: APPROXIMATELY 1 CUP

VINAIGRETTE DRESSING

1/4 CUP BALSAMIC VINEGAR

1 TEASPOON PREPARED DIJON MUSTARD

1/4 TEASPOON SALT   1 CUP OLIVE OIL

FRESHLY GROUND BLACK PEPPER TO TASTE

COMBINE INGREDIENTS AND SHAKE VIGOROUSLY IN SCREW-TOP JAR.

YIELD: 1 1/4 CUPS

FISH
SHELLFISH

FISH • SHELLFISH

FOILED SHRIMP

8 MEDIUM SHRIMP, COOKED, SHELLED, AND DEVEINED
2 TABLESPOONS CHOPPED SCALLIONS OR ONIONS
12 CARROT STRIPS   1/4 CLOVE MINCED GARLIC
1 TABLESPOON TERIYAKI OR SOY SAUCE
THIN SLICES OF WATER CHESTNUTS, CELERY, AND/OR
CHINESE SNOW PEAS

1. ARRANGE SHRIMP WITH THE OTHER INGREDIENTS IN CENTER OF A SQUARE OF ALUMINUM FOIL. BRING UP FOIL AND PINCH TOP AND SIDES TO MAKE A TIGHT BAG. REFRIGERATE UNTIL READY TO BAKE.

2. PLACE ON SHALLOW PAN AND BAKE FOR 15 TO 20 MINUTES AT 400°F.

3. SERVE WITH RICE. MAKE ADDITIONAL SOY SAUCE AVAILABLE.

YIELD: 1 SERVING

THIS IS AN IDEAL DINNER FOR FAMILIES WHO ARE CAUGHT UP IN THE HUSTLE AND BUSTLE OF EVERYDAY LIFE. SINCE BAGS ARE INDIVIDUALIZED, THEY CAN BE POPPED IN THE OVEN ANYTIME TO FIT THE SCHEDULE OF A BUSY PERSON.

DIJON BROILED FLOUNDER FILLETS [L]

8 SMALL SKINLESS, BONELESS FLOUNDER FILLETS (ABOUT 2 POUNDS)

3 TABLESPOONS MAYONNAISE

2 TABLESPOONS DIJON MUSTARD

2 TEASPOONS CHOPPED PARSLEY

LEMON WEDGES

1. PREHEAT BROILER. OIL A BAKING SHEET OR DISH AND ARRANGE FILLETS IN SINGLE LAYER.

2. BLEND MAYONNAISE, MUSTARD, AND PARSLEY. BRUSH MIXTURE EVENLY OVER THE FILLETS. PLACE FILLETS 3 TO 4 INCHES FROM BROILER. BROIL ABOUT 5 TO 10 MINUTES OR UNTIL GOLDEN BROWN ON TOP AND FISH FLAKES EASILY WITH FORK. SERVE WITH LEMON WEDGES.

YIELD: 4 TO 6 SERVINGS

SOLE MAY BE SUBSTITUTED FOR FLOUNDER BUT BROILING TIME WILL BE SHORTER (PROBABLY 4 TO 7 MINUTES).

CAN-CAN BOUILLABAISSE [L]

2 MEDIUM POTATOES

2 ONIONS, COARSELY CHOPPED

2 GREEN PEPPERS

1 BAY LEAF

2 FRESH GARLIC CLOVES

1/3 CUP MINCED PARSLEY

32 OUNCES STEWED TOMATOES

1 TEASPOON ITALIAN HERBS

2 8-OUNCE CANS TOMATO SAUCE

1/2 TEASPOON SALT OR TO TASTE

2 CARROTS, COARSELY CHOPPED

1/4 TEASPOON GROUND BLACK PEPPER

10 OUNCES FROZEN ITALIAN GREEN BEANS (OPTIONAL)

1 CAN CHICK-PEAS (OPTIONAL)

2 1/2 POUNDS HADDOCK, OR ANY FIRM-FLESHED FISH

1/2 POUND FRESH COOKED, PEELED, AND DEVEINED SHRIMP

6 1/2-OUNCE CAN CHOPPED OR WHOLE CLAMS, UNDRAINED

1. PEEL AND CUT POTATOES INTO 1/2-INCH PIECES. SEED AND CHOP GREEN PEPPERS. MINCE GARLIC.

2. COMBINE FIRST 14 INGREDIENTS IN 3-QUART SAUCEPAN AND BRING TO BOIL OVER MEDIUM-HIGH HEAT. REDUCE HEAT, COVER, AND SIMMER UNTIL VEGETABLES ARE ALMOST TENDER, ABOUT 30 MINUTES.

3. ADD FISH (CUT INTO LARGE PIECES), SHRIMP, AND CLAMS. CONTINUE SIMMERING UNTIL FISH FLAKES EASILY WITH FORK, ABOUT 10 MINUTES. TASTE AND ADJUST SEASONING.

4. THE BROTH AND VEGGIES CAN BE PREPARED AHEAD, THEN REHEATED, AND THE FISH ADDED ABOUT 1/2 HOUR BEFORE SERVING.

YIELD: 6 TO 8 SERVINGS

THIS IS A WONDERFUL DINNER SERVED WITH CRUSTY ITALIAN BREAD AND A DESSERT OF FRUIT AND ASSORTED CHEESE.

SCALLOPS MORNAY FLORENTINE [B, M]

2 POUNDS SEA SCALLOPS CUT INTO 4 PIECES OR WHOLE BAY SCALLOPS
4 TABLESPOONS BUTTER   1 CUP SCALLOP COOKING LIQUID
4 TABLESPOONS FLOUR   1 CUP **WHOLE OR SKIM** EVAPORATED MILK
1 CUP GRATED CHEDDAR CHEESE
1 TABLESPOON SHERRY, OPTIONAL
2 10-OUNCE PACKAGES FROZEN, CHOPPED SPINACH
1 CUP COARSELY CRUSHED CORNFLAKES

1. RINSE SCALLOPS. IN MICROWAVE OR ON STOVE TOP, POACH SCALLOPS IN WATER UNTIL OPAQUE, ABOUT 2 TO 4 MINUTES DEPENDING ON MICROWAVE WATTAGE. DRAIN AND RESERVE 1 CUP OF THIS COOKING LIQUID FOR THE SAUCE (THIS IS PREFERABLE TO USING AN ALL-MILK SAUCE). BUTTER SCALLOP SHELLS OR RAMEKINS.

2. MELT BUTTER IN MICROWAVE. BLEND IN FLOUR AND RETURN TO MICROWAVE. COOK FOR 1 MINUTE. GRADUALLY ADD COOKING LIQUID AND MILK. COOK UNTIL THICKENED, STIRRING ONCE EVERY MINUTE, FOR ABOUT 4 MINUTES. REMOVE FROM MICROWAVE.

3. ADD CHEESE. RETURN TO MICROWAVE FOR 30 SECONDS OR UNTIL CHEESE IS MELTED. ADD OPTIONAL SHERRY. IF SAUCE IS LUMPY, RUN IT IN THE BLENDER UNTIL SMOOTH. ADD SCALLOPS AND SET ASIDE.

4. COOK SPINACH IN MICROWAVE FOR ABOUT A MINUTE LESS THAN DIRECTED ON PACKAGE. DRAIN THOROUGHLY, SQUEEZING OUT ALL EXCESS LIQUID. PLACE IN BOTTOM OF SCALLOP SHELLS OR RAMEKINS.

(CONTINUED ON NEXT PAGE)

SCALLOPS MORNAY FLORENTINE [B, M] *(CONTINUED)*

5. PLACE SCALLOP MIXTURE ON TOP OF SPINACH. COVER WITH CRUSHED CORNFLAKES.

6. BAKE AT 400°F FOR 10 MINUTES OR UNTIL BROWN AND BUBBLY.

YIELD: 4 TO 6 SERVINGS

*THIS CAN BE PREPARED AHEAD AND REFRIGERATED UNTIL BAKING TIME (ALLOW MORE BAKING TIME WHEN REFRIGERATED). SERVE WITH GREEN PEAS OR ASPARAGUS, **TOMATO ASPIC SALAD**, AND ROLLS. HOW ABOUT A DESSERT OF **LEMON CAKE PIE**?*

HERB GARDENER'S QUICK FILLET OF SOLE [L]

6 FILLETS OF SOLE
3 TABLESPOONS SAUTERNE WINE
SALT AND FRESHLY GROUND PEPPER
3 TABLESPOONS SLIVERED ALMONDS
1 TABLESPOON EACH FRESH PARSLEY, CHERVIL, AND CHIVES

1. BUTTER A SHALLOW BAKING DISH AND LAY FILLETS IN DISH.

2. DRIZZLE WINE OVER FISH. SEASON WITH SALT AND PEPPER. SPRINKLE WITH PARSLEY, CHERVIL, AND CHIVES. TOP WITH SLIVERED ALMONDS.

3. BAKE AT 400°F UNTIL FISH FLAKES EASILY, OR ABOUT 10 MINUTES.

YIELD: 4 SERVINGS

KITTY'S CRABMEAT MORNAY [M]

3 TABLESPOONS BUTTER   1/4 POUND CHEDDAR CHEESE
3 TABLESPOONS FLOUR   1 SMALL CAN BUTTON MUSHROOMS
1/2 CUP WHOLE MILK   1 CAN CRABMEAT OR 1/2 POUND CRAB BLEND
EVAPORATED MILK TO MAKE 1 CUP WHEN ADDED TO MUSHROOM LIQUID
1 TO 2 TABLESPOONS SHERRY, OPTIONAL
BUTTERED BREAD CRUMBS

1. RINSE AND DRAIN CRABMEAT. MELT BUTTER IN 1-QUART MICROWAVE BOWL. STIR IN FLOUR AND COOK FOR 30 SECONDS. GRADUALLY ADD MILK AND MUSHROOM JUICE/EVAPORATED MILK MIXTURE. RUN ON HIGH IN MICROWAVE AND STIR EVERY 30 SECONDS UNTIL THICKENED.

2. ADD GRATED CHEESE. STIR UNTIL MELTED. ADD MUSHROOMS, CRABMEAT, AND OPTIONAL SHERRY. PLACE IN LARGE BUTTERED SCALLOP SHELLS OR RAMEKINS AND TOP WITH BUTTERED CRUMBS. BAKE AT 350°F FOR 15 MINUTES.

YIELD: 4 SERVINGS

*IF YOU KEEP CANS OF CRABMEAT, EVAPORATED MILK, AND MUSHROOMS IN YOUR PANTRY, YOU'LL ALWAYS BE READY FOR LAST-MINUTE GUESTS. SERVE WITH **TOMATO ASPIC SALAD** AND ROLLS. CRABMEAT MORNAY IS EASY TO MAKE YET SOPHISTICATED.*

FLOUNDER FILLET d'LITE [M]

2 POUNDS FLAT FISH (FILLET OF FLOUNDER OR SOLE)
1 MEDIUM ONION   1/2 POUND CRAB BLEND
3 TO 4 TABLESPOONS WHITE WINE   1/3 CUP LITE SOUR CREAM
1/4 TEASPOON FRESHLY GROUND PEPPER   1/3 CUP LITE MAYONNAISE
1/2 CUP SHREDDED SHARP LITE CHEESE (OPTIONAL)

1. THINLY SLICE ONION. SEPARATE AND SPREAD OVER BOTTOM OF OVENPROOF OR MICROWAVE-SAFE DISH.

2. RINSE FISH, AND SPLIT DOWN MIDDLE AND REMOVE CARTILAGE (SPINY STRIP).

3. LAY FISH ON TOP OF ONIONS. SPRINKLE WITH WINE AND FRESHLY GROUND PEPPER.

4. CUT UP CRAB BLEND IN SMALLER THAN BITE-SIZED PIECES. MIX WITH SOUR CREAM AND MAYONNAISE. SPREAD ON FISH FILLETS.

5. BAKE AT 375°F FOR 20 TO 25 MINUTES OR MICROWAVE ON HIGH FOR 6 TO 7 MINUTES.

6. ADD CHEESE, IF DESIRED, AND BROIL IN OVEN FOR 2 TO 3 MINUTES.

YIELD: 4 TO 5 SERVINGS

HERBED SCALLOPS

2 POUNDS FRESH SCALLOPS
1/4 CUP BUTTER
1/4 CUP CHOPPED PARSLEY

2 TABLESPOONS CHOPPED BASIL
1 TEASPOON SALT
1/4 TEASPOON FRESHLY GROUND PEPPER

1. WASH SCALLOPS. IF USING SEA SCALLOPS, CUT IN HALF OR QUARTERS.

2. MELT BUTTER IN OVENPROOF BAKING DISH AND ADD SCALLOPS. SPRINKLE WITH REMAINING INGREDIENTS.

3. BAKE 15 TO 20 MINUTES AT 350°F, STIRRING OCCASIONALLY. SERVE SAUCE OVER SCALLOPS. GARNISH WITH LEMON WEDGES.

YIELD: 4 TO 6 SERVINGS

THIS RECIPE CAN BE ASSEMBLED AHEAD OF TIME, REFRIGERATED, AND BAKED JUST PRIOR TO SERVING.

SCALLOPS IN SOUR CREAM CAPER SAUCE [M]

1 POUND BAY SCALLOPS OR QUARTERED SEA SCALLOPS
1/2 CUP DRY WHITE WINE (I.E., CHABLIS, FRENCH COLUMBARD)
1/2 CUP SOUR CREAM   1/2 CUP MAYONNAISE
2 TABLESPOONS CAPERS OR FRESH CHOPPED DILL

1. RINSE SCALLOPS AND CHECK FOR BITS OF SHELL. POACH OR SIMMER IN WINE IN MICROWAVE-SAFE DISH OR ON STOVE. SCALLOPS ARE DONE IN 5 TO 6 MINUTES OR WHEN OPAQUE.

2. DRAIN. COVER AND REFRIGERATE OVERNIGHT OR UNTIL THOROUGHLY CHILLED.

3. COMBINE SOUR CREAM, MAYONNAISE, AND CAPERS. SERVE CHILLED SCALLOPS TOPPED WITH CREAMY CAPER SAUCE ON A LETTUCE LEAF.

YIELD: 6 APPETIZER OR 3 MEAL-SIZE SERVINGS

*FOR DINNER ON A HOT SUMMER EVENING, SERVE WITH **TOMATO ASPIC SALAD**, HOT ROLLS, AND MAYBE LEMON SHERBET AND COOKIES FOR DESSERT.*

SCALLOPS BROCHETTE

1 POUND SEA SCALLOPS OR LARGE BAY SCALLOPS
13 1/2-OUNCE CAN OR FRESH PINEAPPLE CHUNKS (DRAIN IF CANNED)
1 GREEN PEPPER, CUT IN 1-INCH SQUARES

1/2 POUND MUSHROOMS	1/4 CUP CHOPPED PARSLEY
1/2 POUND CHERRY TOMATOES	1/4 CUP SOY SAUCE
1/4 CUP OIL	1/2 TEASPOON SALT
1/4 CUP LEMON JUICE	DASH BLACK PEPPER

1. PLACE SCALLOPS, PINEAPPLE, GREEN PEPPER, MUSHROOMS, AND CHERRY TOMATOES IN BOWL. COMBINE OIL, LEMON JUICE, PARSLEY, SOY SAUCE, SALT, AND PEPPER. POUR SAUCE OVER MIXTURE AND LET STAND 30 MINUTES, STIRRING OCCASIONALLY.

2. USING LONG SKEWERS, ALTERNATE FISH, PINEAPPLE, MUSHROOMS, GREEN PEPPER, AND CHERRY TOMATOES UNTIL SKEWERS ARE FILLED.

3. IN OVEN BROILER OR OUTDOOR GRILL, PLACE BROCHETTES ABOUT 4 INCHES FROM SOURCE OF HEAT, BASTING WITH SAUCE. TURN AND COOK 5 TO 7 MINUTES OR UNTIL DONE AND SCALLOPS BECOME OPAQUE.

YIELD: 4 TO 6 SERVINGS

*PLACED ON A BED OF WHITE RICE ACCOMPANIED BY A MIXED GREEN SALAD, **SCALLOPS BROCHETTE** IS A DELICIOUSLY UNIQUE DINNER.*

YOGI'S QUICK FISH [L, M]

1/2 SWEET ONION OR 1/2 PEELED CUCUMBER, SLICED
1 POUND FLOUNDER, SOLE, HADDOCK, ORANGE ROUGHY,
SWORDFISH, OR SALMON
1/4 CUP WHITE WINE   FRESHLY GROUND PEPPER TO TASTE
1 TABLESPOON BUTTER (OPTIONAL)

1. ARRANGE ONION OR CUCUMBER IN BOTTOM OF MICROWAVE-SAFE DISH (WITH COVER). CUCUMBER GOES BEST WITH SALMON.

2. PLACE FISH FILLETS ON TOP.

3. POUR WINE OVER FISH. SPRINKLE WITH PEPPER. DOT WITH BUTTER, IF DESIRED.

4. MICROWAVE, COVERED, ON HIGH FOR 6 TO 7 MINUTES OR UNTIL FISH FLAKES OR TURNS OPAQUE, DEPENDING ON WHICH FISH IS USED.

YIELD: 3 SERVINGS

*SERVE WITH **CUCUMBER-DILL DRESSING**, OR A TARTAR SAUCE MADE OF 1/3 CUP MAYONNAISE WITH 1 TEASPOON PREPARED MUSTARD AND 1 TABLESPOON DRAINED PICKLED RELISH.*

PASTA WITH WHITE CLAM SAUCE

13 OUNCES CANNED CHOPPED CLAMS

3 CLOVES GARLIC, HALVED

1 CUP COARSELY CHOPPED ONIONS

1/2 CUP OLIVE OR SALAD OIL

1/2 CUP BUTTER

2 TABLESPOONS SNIPPED PARSLEY

1 POUND LINGUINI OR SPAGHETTI

1/2 CUP GRATED PARMESAN CHEESE

1. DRAIN CLAMS, RESERVING JUICE.

2. SAUTÉ GARLIC AND ONIONS IN OIL AND BUTTER. COOK UNTIL ONIONS ARE SOFT AND GARLIC IS GOLDEN. DISCARD GARLIC. ADD RESERVED CLAM LIQUID AND SIMMER, UNCOVERED, FOR 10 MINUTES OR UNTIL REDUCED ABOUT ONE-THIRD IN VOLUME. ADD PARSLEY, CHOPPED CLAMS, SALT, AND PEPPER TO TASTE AND SIMMER FOR AN ADDITIONAL 2 MINUTES.

3. COOK PASTA AS LABEL DIRECTS. DRAIN THOROUGHLY AND ARRANGE ON HEATED PLATES.

4. LADLE WHITE CLAM SAUCE OVER PASTA AND SERVE WITH GRATED PARMESAN CHEESE.

YIELD: 4 SERVINGS

SERVE WITH TOSSED SALAD AND CRISP ITALIAN BREAD.

TRADITIONALLY, WHITE CLAM SAUCE IS SERVED WITH LINGUINI. HOWEVER, WE HAVE FOUND THAT THIS SAUCE CAN BE SERVED QUITE SUCCESSFULLY WITH ROTINI OR ROTELLI, A CORKSCREW-SHAPED PASTA. WE ACTUALLY PREFER IT THAT WAY AS THE PASTA ABSORBS THE SAUCE AND IS EASIER TO SPEAR ON THE FORK... NO WINDING REQUIRED!

POULTRY

POULTRY

HINT:

RINSE AND DRY CHICKEN BEFORE STARTING EACH RECIPE.

ELEGANT CHICKEN BREASTS WITH ARTICHOKES

4 BONELESS, SKINLESS CHICKEN BREASTS, SPLIT

1/2 POUND FRESH MUSHROOMS

1 TEASPOON SALT

1/4 TEASPOON GROUND PEPPER

1 TEASPOON PAPRIKA

1/2 CUP BUTTER

2 TABLESPOONS FLOUR

2/3 CUP CHICKEN BOUILLON

3 TABLESPOONS SHERRY

2 JARS MARINATED ARTICHOKE HEARTS, DRAINED

1. SLICE OR QUARTER MUSHROOMS. SPRINKLE CHICKEN WITH SALT, PEPPER, AND PAPRIKA. BROWN CHICKEN IN 1/4 CUP BUTTER. TRANSFER FROM PAN TO OVENPROOF CASSEROLE.

2. ADD ANOTHER 1/4 CUP OF BUTTER TO THE SKILLET AND SAUTÉ MUSHROOMS FOR 5 MINUTES. SPRINKLE WITH FLOUR. STIR IN THE BOUILLON AND SHERRY; SIMMER 5 MINUTES MORE.

3. ARRANGE ARTICHOKE HEARTS AMONG CHICKEN PIECES AND POUR MUSHROOM MIXTURE OVER ALL. COVER AND BAKE AT 375°F FOR 45 MINUTES.

YIELD: 4 TO 6 SERVINGS

*ACCOMPANY THIS CHICKEN DISH WITH RICE, **FANCY SHREDDED CARROTS**, AND A SALAD OF CHILLED ASPARAGUS SPEARS.*

SOUR CREAM–LEMON CHICKEN

3 POUNDS BONELESS, SKINLESS CHICKEN BREASTS

1/4 CUP BUTTER	1/4 TEASPOON PEPPER
1/2 POUND MUSHROOMS	2 TABLESPOONS CHOPPED PARSLEY
2 TABLESPOONS FLOUR	4 CHOPPED SCALLIONS
2 CUPS SOUR CREAM	2 TABLESPOONS GRATED LEMON RIND
1 1/2 TEASPOONS SALT	3 TABLESPOONS FRESH LEMON JUICE

1. MELT BUTTER AND BROWN CHICKEN IN A FRYING PAN. REMOVE CHICKEN AND PLACE IN CASSEROLE.

2. QUARTER OR SLICE MUSHROOMS AND SAUTÉ LIGHTLY IN FRYING PAN, ADDING MORE BUTTER IF NECESSARY. TRANSFER SAUTÉED MUSHROOMS TO CASSEROLE.

3. STIR FLOUR INTO THE PAN JUICES. ADD SOUR CREAM, SALT, AND PEPPER AND MIX WELL. SIMMER FOR 3 MINUTES UNTIL SAUCE THICKENS.

4. STIR IN ALL REMAINING INGREDIENTS EXCEPT LEMON JUICE. POUR OVER CHICKEN AND MUSHROOMS. BAKE COVERED AT 350°F FOR 1 HOUR OR UNTIL CHICKEN IS TENDER.

5. REMOVE CHICKEN AND PLACE ON A PLATTER. STIR LEMON JUICE INTO THE PAN JUICES AND POUR OVER CHICKEN TO SERVE.

YIELD: 6 SERVINGS

THIS RECIPE MAY BE PREPARED EARLIER IN THE DAY, REFRIGERATED, AND THEN BAKED ABOUT AN HOUR BEFORE SERVING.

CHICKEN GLAZED WITH HONEY AND LEMON [L+]

3 POUNDS SKINLESS, BONELESS CHICKEN BREASTS OR THIGHS
1/2 CUP FLOUR   1/8 TEASPOON PEPPER
3/4 TEASPOON SALT   1/4 CUP BUTTER

GLAZE

1 CUP HONEY   1/2 CUP LEMON JUICE
        1 TEASPOON GRATED LEMON RIND (OPTIONAL)

1. SET OVEN TO 350°F. SHAKE CHICKEN IN A MIXTURE OF FLOUR, SALT, AND PEPPER. MELT BUTTER IN LARGE SKILLET AND LIGHTLY BROWN CHICKEN PIECES. REMOVE TO BAKING DISH.

2. COMBINE INGREDIENTS FOR GLAZE. POUR GLAZE OVER CHICKEN AND BAKE FOR 45 MINUTES, BASTING FREQUENTLY. THE SAUCE WILL THICKEN AS THE CHICKEN BAKES. TURN OVEN UP TO 400°F AND CONTINUE BAKING UNTIL CHICKEN IS GOLDEN BROWN.

YIELD: 6 SERVINGS

THIS IS MY MOTHER-IN-LAW'S FAVORITE CHICKEN DISH!

EAST INDIAN CURRIED CHICKEN [L+]

3 POUNDS BONELESS, SKINLESS CHICKEN BREASTS

1/2 CUP FLOUR	1/2 GREEN PEPPER, CHOPPED
1 1/2 TEASPOONS SALT	1/2 CLOVE GARLIC, MINCED
1/2 TEASPOON GROUND PEPPER	1 QUART PLUM TOMATOES
1/4 CUP PEANUT OIL	1 1/2 TEASPOONS CURRY
1 LARGE ONION	1/2 CUP RAISINS

1/2 CHOPPED, PEELED APPLE

SHREDDED COCONUT, CHOPPED CASHEWS, AND **APPLE CHUTNEY**

1. CUT EACH BREAST IN ABOUT 6 PIECES. DREDGE CHICKEN IN COMBINATION OF FLOUR, SALT, AND PEPPER. BROWN PIECES IN PEANUT OIL. ADD MORE OIL AS NECESSARY. TRANSFER TO DUTCH OVEN OR OVENPROOF CASSEROLE DISH.

2. SAUTÉ ONION, GREEN PEPPER, AND MINCED GARLIC. ADD TOMATOES, CURRY, AND RAISINS TO SAUTÉED MIXTURE AND SIMMER A FEW MINUTES. POUR MIXTURE OVER CHICKEN.

3. BAKE COVERED 1 HOUR AT 350°F. ADD CHOPPED APPLE AND BAKE AN ADDITIONAL 15 MINUTES.

YIELD: 4 TO 6 SERVINGS

SERVE OVER WHITE RICE ACCOMPANIED BY COCONUT, CASHEWS, AND **APPLE CHUTNEY.** **INDONESIAN CUCUMBERS** *IS A GOOD SIDE DISH WITH THIS RECIPE.*

CHICKEN DIJON MOUTARDE

4 BONELESS, SKINLESS CHICKEN BREASTS, SPLIT

6 TABLESPOONS BUTTER	1/4 CUP DRY WHITE WINE
1/4 CUP DIJON MUSTARD	1 CHICKEN BOUILLON CUBE
2 CUPS BREAD CRUMBS	1 CLOVE MINCED GARLIC

1 TABLESPOON CHOPPED, FRESH PARSLEY

1. SET OVEN TO 350°F. MELT 4 TABLESPOONS OF BUTTER IN SKILLET. BROWN CHICKEN ON BOTH SIDES. REMOVE BREASTS FROM PAN.

2. COAT BOTH SIDES OF CHICKEN WITH DIJON MUSTARD.

3. DIP EACH PIECE IN BREAD CRUMBS. PLACE IN BUTTERED BAKING DISH IN A SINGLE LAYER AND DOT EACH PIECE WITH BUTTER.

4. COVER AND BAKE FOR 15 MINUTES. UNCOVER AND CONTINUE BAKING FOR ANOTHER 15 MINUTES OR UNTIL DONE.

5. MEANWHILE, ADD WHITE WINE TO PAN AND SCRAPE ALL JUICES AND BITS THAT ARE ATTACHED. THIS IS KNOWN AS DEGLAZING. DISSOLVE CHICKEN BOUILLON CUBE IN 1/2 CUP BOILING WATER. ADD TO PAN WITH GARLIC AND PARSLEY. REDUCE TO 1/4 CUP. ADD REMAINING 2 TABLESPOONS OF BUTTER. SWIRL IN PAN UNTIL BUTTER IS MELTED. POUR OVER CHICKEN BREASTS.

YIELD: 4 SERVINGS

*TO COMPLETE THIS DINNER, SERVE **CHICKEN DIJON MOUTARDE** WITH WILD RICE, ASPARAGUS, AND A SALAD MADE WITH PINEAPPLE CHUNKS.*

EASY ITALIAN BAKED CHICKEN [L+]

6 BONELESS, SKINLESS CHICKEN BREASTS AND/OR THIGHS
1/2 TO 1 BOTTLE ITALIAN DRESSING

1. PLACE CHICKEN IN A 9 X 13-INCH BAKING PAN.

2. POUR DRESSING OVER CHICKEN. BE SURE TO COAT ALL SIDES.

3. POP IN OVEN AND BAKE AT 350°F FOR 45 MINUTES OR UNTIL DONE.

YIELD: 6 SERVINGS

YOU MIGHT SERVE THIS ITALIAN CHICKEN WITH A SIDE DISH OF **GREEN FETTUCINE WITH CHEESE AND MUSHROOMS**, *A TOSSED SALAD, AND CRUSTY ITALIAN BREAD.*

MEATS

MEATS

SIMPLE BEEF-VEGETABLE STEW [L]

3 POUNDS STEWING BEEF, CUBED

ENOUGH OIL TO BROWN MEAT

1 LARGE CAN TOMATOES

1 PACKAGE FROZEN PEAS

6 CARROTS, CUT IN HALF OR THIRDS

3 MEDIUM POTATOES, CUBED

3 MEDIUM ONIONS, QUARTERED

1 CUP SLICED CELERY

1/4 CUP RED WINE

1 TEASPOON SUGAR

3 TABLESPOONS QUICK-COOKING TAPIOCA

GENEROUS GRINDING OF BLACK PEPPER

1 TEASPOON SALT AND PINCHES OF THYME, MARJORAM, AND ROSEMARY

1. SET OVEN TO 225°F. BROWN MEAT IN OIL.

2. PLACE BROWNED MEAT AND REMAINING INGREDIENTS IN A DUTCH OVEN. COVER TIGHTLY AND BAKE FOR 5 HOURS.

YIELD: 8 SERVINGS

IF BROWNING MEAT IS DIFFICULT, SKIP IT; IT REALLY ISN'T ALL THAT NECESSARY. SERVE WITH CRUSTY FRENCH BREAD WITH GARLIC BUTTER.

NEW ENGLAND BOILED DINNER

1 HAM BUTT (USUALLY 2 TO 2 1/2 POUNDS)

4 CARROTS	4 POTATOES
4 SMALL TO MEDIUM ONIONS	1 POUND FRESH GREEN BEANS

1/2 TO 3/4 POUND FRESH OR FROZEN BRUSSELS SPROUTS

1. PLACE HAM IN LARGE HEAVY KETTLE OR DUTCH OVEN. ADD WATER UNTIL IT REACHES MIDWAY ON THE HAM. COVER AND **JUST SIMMER** FOR 1 HOUR ON TOP OF STOVE.

2. ADD CARROTS, ONIONS, AND POTATOES. COOK FOR 20 ADDITIONAL MINUTES.

3. ADD GREEN BEANS. COOK FOR 30 MINUTES MORE.

4. COOK BRUSSELS SPROUTS IN SAUCEPAN ON STOVE TOP.

5. WHILE BRUSSELS SPROUTS ARE COOKING, REMOVE HAM FROM POT AND CUT INTO 1/4-INCH-THICK SLICES.

YIELD: 4 SERVINGS

ARRANGE SLICED HAM, POTATOES, CARROTS, ONIONS, AND GREEN BEANS ON LARGE SERVING PLATTER. MAKE DIJON MUSTARD AVAILABLE FOR THE HAM AND HAVE BRUSSELS SPROUTS IN A SIDE DISH. THIS DINNER NEEDS ONLY CORN MUFFINS TO COMPLETE IT AND SPICY IRISH APPLE CRISP AS THE FINISHING TOUCH.

SHORTCUT LASAGNE

1/2 CUP PARSLEY OR SPINACH

1/4 CUP PARMESAN CHEESE

1 EGG

12 OUNCES COTTAGE CHEESE

1/4 POUND EACH SWEET ITALIAN AND HOT ITALIAN SAUSAGE

1 POUND GROUND BEEF

24 OUNCES VEGETABLE JUICE

1 TABLESPOON VEGETABLE OIL

15 OUNCES TOMATO SAUCE

15 OUNCES PLUM TOMATOES

1 POUND LASAGNE NOODLES

2 ENVELOPES SPAGHETTI SAUCE MIX

8 OUNCES MOZZARELLA CHEESE

1. SET OVEN TO 350°F. OIL 9 X 13-INCH BAKING DISH.

2. CHOP PARSLEY OR SPINACH. COMBINE WITH EGG, PARMESAN CHEESE, AND COTTAGE CHEESE AND SET ASIDE.

3. REMOVE SAUSAGE FROM CASING. BROWN GROUND BEEF AND CRUMBLED SAUSAGE IN OIL. POUR OFF EXCESS FAT. COMBINE TOMATOES, SPAGHETTI SAUCE MIX, VEGETABLE JUICE, AND TOMATO SAUCE. BRING TO A BOIL AND SIMMER FOR 10 MINUTES.

4. COVER BOTTOM OF BAKING DISH WITH THIN LAYER OF MEAT SAUCE. ADD LAYER OF **UNCOOKED** LASAGNE NOODLES, HALF THE COTTAGE CHEESE MIXTURE, ANOTHER LAYER OF NOODLES, AND THEN HALF THE MEAT SAUCE. REPEAT LAYERS, ENDING WITH MEAT SAUCE. SPRINKLE WITH MOZZARELLA CHEESE.

5. COVER TIGHTLY WITH ALUMINUM FOIL. SET ON TRAY AND BAKE FOR 1 HOUR. REMOVE AND LET STAND 15 MINUTES BEFORE SERVING.

YIELD: 6 TO 8 SERVINGS

SERVE WITH A SALAD AND GARLIC BREAD. VEGETARIANS COULD REPLACE MEAT WITH ONIONS, PEPPERS, AND MUSHROOMS.

GUINNESS IRISH STEW

1 SLICE BACON, CUT INTO 1/2-INCH PIECES

2 POUNDS LEAN STEWING BEEF, CUT INTO 1 1/2-INCH PIECES

1 LARGE ONION, CHOPPED	1 1/2 CUPS MEAT STOCK
2 TABLESPOONS FLOUR	6 1/2 OUNCES GUINNESS STOUT BEER
2 CARROTS, SLICED	2 TABLESPOONS DARK BROWN SUGAR
12 SMALL WHITE ONIONS	2 TABLESPOONS RED WINE VINEGAR

BOUQUET GARNI

(THYME, PARSLEY SPRIGS, BAY LEAF, TIED IN A CHEESECLOTH BAG)

COARSE SALT AND FRESHLY GROUND PEPPER TO TASTE

1. SET OVEN TO 350°F.

2. HEAT OIL IN A HEAVY CASSEROLE THAT WILL GO BOTH ON TOP OF STOVE AND INSIDE OVEN. ADD BACON AND FRY UNTIL BROWNED. REMOVE BACON. DRAIN ON PAPER TOWELS.

3. DRY CUBES OF BEEF WITH PAPER TOWELS. BROWN CUBES IN CASSEROLE, A FEW AT A TIME. REMOVE AND ADD CHOPPED ONION. BROWN LIGHTLY. STIR IN FLOUR AND COOK FOR 2 OR 3 MINUTES WITHOUT BURNING. RETURN BEEF WITH ITS JUICES AND BACON TO CASSEROLE. ADD CARROTS, WHITE ONIONS, STOCK, BEER, SUGAR, VINEGAR, BOUQUET GARNI, SALT, AND PEPPER. BRING TO A BOIL.

4. COVER, TRANSFER TO OVEN, AND BAKE FOR 1 1/2 TO 2 HOURS, STIRRING OCCASIONALLY. REMOVE GARNI, SEASON TO TASTE, AND SERVE.

YIELD: 4 SERVINGS

(CONTINUED ON NEXT PAGE)

GUINNESS IRISH STEW (CONTINUED)

*SERVE THIS WITH PARSLEY-BUTTERED, BOILED RED-SKINNED POTATOES, A SALAD OF GREENS, AND LOTS OF BREAD WITH BUTTER. TO FINISH OFF THE DINNER, GO ALL IRISH WITH **SPICY IRISH APPLE CRISP.***

ORANGE BAKED PORK CHOPS

6 THICK PORK CHOPS
1/2 CUP ORANGE JUICE
1 TEASPOON SALT

1/4 TEASPOON PEPPER
1/2 TEASPOON DRY MUSTARD
1/4 CUP BROWN SUGAR

1. CUT FAT FROM PORK CHOPS, IF NECESSARY. PLACE CHOPS IN LARGE, SHALLOW BAKING DISH.

2. COMBINE REMAINING INGREDIENTS. POUR OVER CHOPS AND BAKE AT 350°F FOR 1 HOUR (DEPENDING ON THICKNESS OF CHOPS). BASTE OCCASIONALLY DURING BAKING.

YIELD: 4 TO 6 SERVINGS, DEPENDING ON THICKNESS OF CHOPS

*THESE BROWN VERY QUICKLY DURING THE LAST 1/2 HOUR OF BAKING. IF YOU HAVE TO WAIT TO EAT, PUT COVER ON AND ADD MORE JUICE OR WATER. **ORANGE BAKED PORK CHOPS** GO WELL WITH RICE, **FANCY SHREDDED CARROTS**, AND A DESSERT OF **ROCHESTER AUDUBON PIE** OR, IF CRANBERRIES ARE IN SEASON, **CAPE COD APPLE PIE.***

ROAST PEPPERED RIB EYE OF BEEF

5 OR 6 POUND BONELESS RIB EYE BEEF ROAST OR EYE OF THE ROUND
1/2 CUP COARSELY CRACKED PEPPER
1/2 TEASPOON GROUND CARDAMOM SEED
1 TABLESPOON TOMATO PASTE

2 CLOVES MINCED GARLIC   1 CUP SOY SAUCE
1 TEASPOON PAPRIKA   3/4 CUP VINEGAR

1. TRIM FAT FROM BEEF. COMBINE CRACKED PEPPER WITH GROUND CARDAMOM SEED AND PRESS INTO MEAT WITH THE PALM OF YOUR HAND. PLACE IN SHALLOW BAKING PAN.

2. MIX TOMATO PASTE, GARLIC, AND PAPRIKA. GRADUALLY ADD SOY SAUCE AND VINEGAR. POUR OVER MEAT. MARINATE IN THE REFRIGERATOR OVERNIGHT. SPOON MARINADE OVER MEAT SEVERAL TIMES.

3. REMOVE MEAT FROM MARINADE AND LET STAND AT ROOM TEMPERATURE FOR 1 HOUR.

4. WRAP THE MEAT IN FOIL, PLACE IN SHALLOW PAN, AND ROAST AT 300°F FOR 2 HOURS FOR MEDIUM-RARE MEAT. OPEN FOIL; LADLE OUT AND RESERVE DRIPPINGS. BROWN THE ROAST, UNCOVERED, AT 350°F WHILE MAKING THE GRAVY.

5. STRAIN PAN DRIPPINGS AND SKIM OFF EXCESS FAT. SERVE THE ROAST WITH THIS JUICE, OR THICKEN JUICE AS FOLLOWS: BRING 1 CUP MEAT JUICES AND 1 CUP WATER TO BOIL AND SLOWLY ADD 1 1/2 TABLESPOONS CORNSTARCH MIXED WITH 1/4 CUP COLD WATER.

YIELD: 8 TO 10 SERVINGS

(CONTINUED ON NEXT PAGE)

ROAST PEPPERED RIB EYE OF BEEF (CONTINUED)

THERE ARE 2 CUTS OF BEEF THAT CAN BE USED IN THIS RECIPE. ONE IS A RIB EYE. THE LESS EXPENSIVE CUT IS EYE OF THE ROUND. BOTH ARE SUCCESSFUL; WHILE THE RIB EYE IS MORE EXPENSIVE AND TENDER, THE EYE OF THE ROUND IS QUITE SATISFACTORY. TO MAKE A MILDER FLAVORED ROAST, USE LESS PEPPER.

SPICY CRANBERRY POT ROAST [L+]

4 TO 5 POUND BEEF RUMP ROAST, FAT-TRIMMED

2 CUPS FRESH CRANBERRIES

2 CUPS CHOPPED ONIONS

1/2 CUP WATER

1/2 CUP APPLE CIDER

1/2 CUP RED WINE

1/4 CUP SOY SAUCE

1 TEASPOON SALT

2 CLOVES GARLIC, MINCED

1 TEASPOON PUMPKIN PIE SPICE

COARSE PEPPER TO TASTE

1. SET OVEN TO 425°F.

2. ROAST MEAT IN AN UNCOVERED PAN FOR 25 MINUTES. LOWER HEAT TO 350°F.

3. ADD ALL INGREDIENTS TO MEAT. COVER AND BAKE 2 HOURS OR MORE, BASTING OCCASIONALLY WITH PAN JUICES, UNTIL MEAT IS TENDER.

4. REMOVE MEAT AND PLACE ON A CUTTING BOARD. SLICE VERY THIN. SERVE SLICED MEAT WITH PAN JUICES.

YIELD: 8 TO 12 SERVINGS

MARINATED STEAK KABOBS

1 POUND LEAN SIRLOIN STEAK

1 TABLESPOON OLIVE OIL

1 TABLESPOON SHERRY WINE VINEGAR OR RED WINE VINEGAR

1 TABLESPOON MEDIUM-DRY SHERRY

2 TABLESPOONS BEEF BROTH

1 BAY LEAF

1/2 TEASPOON OREGANO

2 MEDIUM ONIONS

16 CHERRY TOMATOES

2 GREEN PEPPERS

1. TRIM ALL EXCESS FAT FROM STEAK. CUT MEAT INTO 1-INCH CUBES. IN A MEDIUM BOWL, COMBINE OLIVE OIL, BAY LEAF, OREGANO, VINEGAR, SHERRY, AND BEEF BROTH. ADD BEEF CUBES AND TUMBLE ABOUT UNTIL WELL-COATED. LET STAND FOR ABOUT 1 HOUR.

2. PREPARE A HOT FIRE IN A GRILL OR PREHEAT BROILER. WHILE GRILL IS HEATING, CUT EACH ONION AND PEPPER INTO 8 SECTIONS.

3. THREAD STEAK, ONIONS, PEPPERS, AND TOMATOES ONTO 4 LONG METAL SKEWERS, ALTERNATING INGREDIENTS.

4. GRILL OR BROIL, TURNING AND BASTING WITH MARINADE SEVERAL TIMES, UNTIL BEEF IS BROWNED OUTSIDE BUT STILL PINK AND JUICY INSIDE, 8 TO 10 MINUTES FOR RARE TO MEDIUM-RARE, OR LONGER IF DESIRED.

YIELD: 4 SERVINGS

CHUCK BOURGUIGNON

6 SLICES BACON, CUT IN HALF, OR 1/2 POUND LINK SAUSAGES
2 1/2 POUNDS BONED CHUCK ROAST (ABOUT 2 INCHES THICK)
3 BEEF BOUILLON CUBES IN 2 CUPS BOILING WATER

1/2 CUP BURGUNDY WINE	2 TABLESPOONS BUTTER
2 LARGE CLOVES GARLIC, MINCED	1/2 POUND SMALL WHITE ONIONS
1 LARGE BAY LEAF	4 MEDIUM CARROTS, HALVED
1/2 POUND FRESH MUSHROOMS	2 TABLESPOONS FLOUR

1. FRY BACON OR LINK SAUSAGES, REMOVE FROM PAN, AND SET ASIDE. RESERVE FAT.

2. TRIM ALL FAT FROM ROAST. CUT ROAST INTO 1 1/2-INCH CUBES.

3. BROWN MEAT IN RESERVED FAT. POUR OFF FAT. SPRINKLE WITH SALT AND PEPPER.

4. ADD BACON OR SAUSAGE LINKS, BEEF BOUILLON, WINE, GARLIC, AND BAY LEAF. COVER AND SIMMER FOR 1 HOUR, STIRRING OCCASIONALLY.

5. AS STEW IS SIMMERING, QUARTER OR THICKLY SLICE MUSHROOMS AND SAUTÉ IN 1 TABLESPOON BUTTER. ADD MUSHROOMS, ONIONS, AND CARROTS TO STEW. COVER AND SIMMER 1 ADDITIONAL HOUR OR UNTIL MEAT IS TENDER. REMOVE BAY LEAF.

6. TO THICKEN, MAKE A PASTE OF FLOUR AND REMAINING TABLESPOON OF BUTTER. BLEND INTO STEW, AND STIR GENTLY UNTIL THICKENED.

YIELD: 4 SERVINGS

BOO'S BOEUF BOURGUIGNON

2 POUNDS TOP ROUND STEAK
1/2 TEASPOON SALT
1/2 TEASPOON PEPPER
DASH OF THYME
1 BUNCH PARSLEY
1/2 BAY LEAF
3 TABLESPOONS OLIVE OIL
2 CUPS RED BURGUNDY WINE

2 TABLESPOONS BRANDY
1/2 POUND LINK SAUSAGES
2 CUPS BEEF BROTH
2 CLOVES GARLIC, MASHED
5 TABLESPOONS FLOUR
1 POUND MUSHROOMS
1/2 PACKAGE FROZEN ONIONS
1 TEASPOON SUGAR

3 TABLESPOONS FLOUR

1. CUT BEEF INTO 3/4-INCH CUBES, REMOVING ALL FAT. PLACE MEAT IN A BOWL. ADD SALT, PEPPER, THYME, PARSLEY, BAY LEAF, OLIVE OIL, WINE, AND BRANDY. MARINATE 48 HOURS IN REFRIGERATOR (MEAT WILL PROBABLY BE GRAY SO STIR AROUND IN MARINADE EVERY TWELVE HOURS OR SO).

2. STRAIN THE MEAT AND DRY, RESERVING THE MARINADE.

3. CUT THE LINK SAUSAGES INTO THIRDS. IN HEAVY DUTCH OVEN, BROWN AND THEN COOK THE SAUSAGES (YOU WILL NOT HAVE TO ADD OIL). REMOVE SAUSAGES AFTER COOKING AND PLACE IN A BOWL.

4. IN THE FAT FROM THE SAUSAGES, BROWN THE MEAT 6 OR 7 PIECES AT A TIME. AS THEY BROWN, REMOVE THEM TO BOWL WITH SAUSAGES. AFTER ALL THE MEAT HAS BEEN THOROUGHLY BROWNED, ADD THE RESERVED MARINADE TO THE DUTCH OVEN AND SCRAPE OR DEGLAZE ALL THE BROWN STUFF ON THE BOTTOM.

5. ADD THE BROWNED SAUSAGE, MEAT, BEEF BROTH, AND GARLIC. BRING TO A BOIL, COVER, AND PUT INTO A 325°F OVEN. THE STEW SHOULD

(CONTINUED ON NEXT PAGE)

BOO'S BOEUF BOURGUIGNON (CONTINUED)

JUST SIMMER SLOWLY IN THE OVEN. COOK FOR 1 1/2 HOURS.

6. IN THE MEANTIME, MELT 2 TABLESPOONS BUTTER AND SAUTÉ THE MUSHROOMS. CUT INTO QUARTERS IF THEY ARE LARGE OR INTO HALVES IF SMALL. SAUTÉ UNTIL COOKED BUT STILL FIRM. REMOVE TO A BOWL.

7. IN SAME PAN, PUT 1/2 CUP WATER AND THE FROZEN ONIONS. COOK FOR 15 MINUTES. POUR OFF WATER, ADD SUGAR AND MORE BUTTER IF NECESSARY. CONTINUE COOKING UNTIL ONIONS ARE GOLDEN BROWN (THE SUGAR DOES THE TRICK). **ALL THE ABOVE IS USUALLY DONE A DAY AHEAD OF TIME.**

8. AFTER THE MEAT IS COOKED AND THE MUSHROOMS AND ONIONS ARE DONE, DRAIN MEAT SAVING ALL THAT SUPER COOKING JUICE. PUT MEAT, ONIONS, AND MUSHROOMS IN COVERED BOWL. CHILL COOKING JUICE AND SCRAPE OFF ANY FAT THAT HAS RISEN.

9. FINALLY, TO FINISH THIS DELIGHTFUL CONCOCTION, PUT ABOUT 3 TABLESPOONS BUTTER IN A LARGE PAN. MELT AND ADD FLOUR. COOK UNTIL MIXTURE BUBBLES AND ADD COOKING JUICE (THERE SHOULD BE ABOUT 4 CUPS). CONTINUE UNTIL **SLIGHTLY** THICKENED. ADD MEAT, ONIONS, AND MUSHROOMS. THERE WILL BE A LITTLE JUICE WITH THE MEAT MIXTURE; ADD THAT, TOO. HEAT THROUGH.

YIELD: 6 SERVINGS

SERVE WITH WILD RICE MIX, SALAD, AND LOTS OF FRENCH BREAD TO SOP UP THAT DELICIOUS GRAVY. THIS RECIPE IS A LITTLE MORE TIME-CONSUMING AND NOT AS EASY AS SOME TO PREPARE, BUT WELL WORTH IT!

LAMB SHISH KABOB

MARINADE:

1/2 CUP SALAD OIL
1/2 CUP OLIVE OIL
DASH OF SALT AND PEPPER
1/3 CUP WINE VINEGAR
1/4 TEASPOON MARJORAM

1/4 TEASPOON THYME
1/2 TEASPOON EACH OREGANO & PAPRIKA
2 TABLESPOONS LEMON JUICE
1 CLOVE GARLIC, CRUSHED
1 TEASPOON DIJON MUSTARD

COMBINE ALL MARINADE INGREDIENTS AND MIX THOROUGHLY.

KABOBS:

2 POUNDS LAMB
2 OR 3 PEPPERS, CUT INTO 1-INCH SQUARES
2 LARGE ONIONS, HALVED AND CUT IN WEDGES
15 CHERRY TOMATOES

1. CUT LAMB IN 1- TO 1 1/2-INCH CUBES.

2. IN REFRIGERATOR, MARINATE LAMB FOR 3 DAYS AND THE VEGETABLES FOR 1 DAY IN MARINADE SAUCE.

3. ARRANGE MEAT AND VEGETABLES ON SKEWERS AND BROIL IN OVEN OR ON OUTDOOR GRILL FOR ABOUT 7 MINUTES, TURNING FREQUENTLY. BRUSH WITH MARINADE, IF NEEDED.

YIELD: 4 TO 6 SERVINGS

THOUGH LAMB IS GREEK, SHISH KABOBS WOULD BE GOOD WITH ITALIAN GREEN BEANS, RICE, AND ROLLS. FINISH WITH FRUIT AND CHEESE.

ORIENTAL-STYLE BROILED LAMB CHOPS

1/4 CUP BROWN SUGAR   1/4 CUP TERIYAKI SAUCE
1 TEASPOON FINELY MINCED FRESH OR CRYSTALLIZED GINGER
6 ROUND BONE OR SHOULDER LAMB CHOPS

1. COMBINE SUGAR, TERIYAKI SAUCE, AND GINGER. PLACE IN A GLASS DISH LARGE ENOUGH TO HOLD LAMB CHOPS IN A SINGLE LAYER.

2. TRIM ANY FAT OFF LAMB CHOPS AND PLACE IN MARINADE. MARINATE FOR AT LEAST 1 HOUR, TURNING CHOPS OVER TO MAKE SURE MARINADE IS ON BOTH SIDES. COVER AND REFRIGERATE.

3. PREHEAT BROILER. DRAIN CHOPS AND PLACE ON SHALLOW METAL PAN. BROIL ABOUT 3 INCHES FROM HEAT SOURCE FOR 3 MINUTES. TURN AND BRUSH EACH PIECE THOROUGHLY WITH MARINADE. BROIL AN ADDITIONAL 3 MINUTES.

YIELD: 3 TO 4 SERVINGS

SERVE WITH FLUFFY WHITE RICE AND GREEN PEAS. LEMON SHERBET, **LEMONY LEMON BARS**, *OR* **LEMON CAKE PIE** *MIGHT BE A SUITABLE FINISH FOR THIS DINNER.*

REUBEN CASSEROLE

1 POUND, 11-OUNCE CAN SAUERKRAUT, WELL-DRAINED

2 MEDIUM TOMATOES, SLICED   2 TABLESPOONS BUTTER

2 TABLESPOONS THOUSAND ISLAND DRESSING

8 OUNCES SLICED CORN BEEF, SHREDDED

2 CUPS SHREDDED SWISS CHEESE

1 CAN FLAKY BISCUITS   1/2 TEASPOON CARAWAY SEEDS

1. SET OVEN TO 425°F.

2. GREASE BOTTOM OF 8- OR 9-INCH SQUARE BAKING PAN. SPREAD SAUERKRAUT IN BOTTOM OF PAN. TOP WITH TOMATO SLICES. DOT WITH BUTTER AND DRESSING. COVER WITH CORNED BEEF. SPRINKLE WITH CHEESE. BAKE FOR 15 MINUTES.

3. REMOVE CASSEROLE FROM OVEN. SEPARATE EACH BISCUIT INTO 3 LAYERS. SLIGHTLY OVERLAP BISCUITS INTO LAYERS TO FORM 3 ROWS. SPRINKLE WITH CARAWAY SEEDS.

4. BAKE FOR 15 TO 20 MINUTES MORE OR UNTIL BISCUITS ARE GOLDEN.

YIELD: 4 TO 6 SERVINGS

VEGETABLES

VEGETABLES

HINTS:

IT'S A GOOD IDEA TO CLIP OFF HERBS AT THE END OF THEIR SEASON AND CHOP AND FREEZE THEM FOR FUTURE USE.

SAUTÉ MUSHROOMS IN BUTTER OR OLIVE OIL. SPRINKLE WITH A LITTLE BASIL WHEN DONE. STORE IN SMALL CONTAINER IN FREEZER FOR USE AT A LATER DATE.

STIR-FRY VEGGIE MEDLEY

6 CUPS SEASONAL FRESH VEGETABLES

2 TABLESPOONS LIGHT PEANUT OIL   1 CUP **STIR-FRY GLAZE**

SUGGESTIONS FOR VEGETABLES:

USE ALL OR ANY COMBINATION OF THE FOLLOWING:

SNOW PEAS

SCALLIONS, CUT IN STRIPS

CARROTS, SLICED

SUMMER SQUASH, SPLIT AND BIAS-SLICED, VERY THIN

FRESH RED PEPPER, CUT INTO STRIPS

FRESH BROCCOLI AND/OR CAULIFLOWER FLORETS

FRESH GREEN BEANS, BIAS-SLICED

MUSHROOMS, SLICED OR QUARTERED

WATER CHESTNUTS, SLICED

1. HEAT PEANUT OIL IN A LARGE SAUTÉ PAN OR WOK UNTIL VERY HOT.

2. ADD VEGETABLES AND TOSS TO HEAT, BUT BE CAREFUL TO RETAIN THEIR CRISPNESS.

3. ADD **STIR-FRY GLAZE** TO VEGETABLES. TOSS AND HEAT THOROUGHLY.

YIELD: 4 TO 6 SERVINGS

FANCY SHREDDED CARROTS [M, F]

2 CUPS SHREDDED CARROTS (APPROXIMATELY 4 TO 6 CARROTS)
1/2 TEASPOON SUGAR   1 TABLESPOON BUTTER
SALT AND PEPPER TO TASTE

1. PLACE CARROTS AND SUGAR IN MICROWAVE-SAFE DISH. COVER AND COOK ON HIGH POWER FOR 2 TO 3 MINUTES, ROTATING DISH HALFWAY THROUGH COOKING TIME.

2. REMOVE FROM MICROWAVE AND STIR. ADD BUTTER AND RETURN TO MICROWAVE FOR ANOTHER HALF-MINUTE. ADD SALT AND PEPPER TO TASTE.

YIELD: 4 SERVINGS

SHREDDED CARROTS USUALLY DO NOT NEED ADDITIONAL WATER FOR MICROWAVE COOKING.

ASPARAGUS CHINOISE

36 ASPARAGUS SPEARS   3 TABLESPOONS SOY SAUCE
1/4 CUP BUTTER   SALT TO TASTE

CUT ASPARAGUS DIAGONALLY IN 1/4-INCH SLICES. SAUTÉ IN BUTTER UNTIL TENDER, ABOUT 6 MINUTES. ABOUT 2 MINUTES BEFORE THE ASPARAGUS IS DONE, ADD SOY SAUCE, AND SALT, TO TASTE.

YIELD: 6 SERVINGS

FRENCH-STYLE MUSHROOMS IN CREAM

1 1/2 POUNDS MUSHROOMS, WASHED AND QUARTERED

2 TABLESPOONS BUTTER	1/3 CUP DRY WHITE WINE
1/2 TEASPOON SALT	1 TEASPOON FLOUR
1/4 TEASPOON FRESHLY GROUND PEPPER	3/4 CUP HEAVY CREAM
JUICE OF 1 LEMON	1/4 TEASPOON NUTMEG

1. MELT BUTTER IN A SKILLET. ADD MUSHROOMS. SEASON WITH SALT, PEPPER, AND LEMON JUICE. COOK OVER MODERATELY HIGH HEAT SO WATER RENDERED FROM THE MUSHROOMS REDUCES QUICKLY.

2. WHEN MOISTURE IS GONE, ADD WINE AND COOK UNTIL LIQUID IS REDUCED TO HALF.

3. SPRINKLE FLOUR OVER MUSHROOMS. MIX WELL. ADD CREAM AND COOK UNTIL SAUCE HAS THICKENED SLIGHTLY. SEASON WITH NUTMEG.

YIELD: 4 TO 6 SERVINGS

*SERVED ON TOAST POINTS, **FRENCH-STYLE MUSHROOMS IN CREAM** MAKES A UNIQUE LUNCHEON DISH. CHERRY TOMATOES WITH TOSSED GREENS WOULD BE COMPLEMENTARY.*

ORANGE-PECAN RICE

1 CUP LONG GRAIN RICE

3 TABLESPOONS BUTTER	1 TEASPOON GRATED ORANGE RIND
1/2 CUP CHOPPED ONION	1 CUP ORANGE JUICE
1 TEASPOON SALT	1 1/4 CUPS WATER
FRESHLY GROUND PEPPER	1/2 CUP CHOPPED PECANS

1. SET OVEN TO 375°F. MELT BUTTER IN A STOVE-TOP, OVENPROOF SKILLET WITH LID. COMBINE LONG GRAIN RICE AND ONION IN SKILLET AND STIR WITH A 2-TINED FORK UNTIL RICE IS GOLDEN BROWN. **NOTE: A 2-TINED FORK KEEPS RICE FROM BECOMING "STICKY."**

2. ADD SALT, PEPPER, GRATED ORANGE RIND, ORANGE JUICE, AND WATER.

3. COVER AND BAKE FOR 45 MINUTES. CHECK AFTER 35 MINUTES. IF RICE SEEMS DRY, ADD MORE WATER; IF TOO MOIST BUT DONE, REMOVE COVER.

4. FINISH BY ADDING COARSELY CHOPPED PECANS AND FLUFFING WITH FORK. ADD MORE BUTTER, IF DESIRED.

YIELD: 4 TO 6 SERVINGS

SERVE THIS WITH A POULTRY DISH!

CELERY ALMONDINE

1/3 CUP BLANCHED ALMONDS
2 TABLESPOONS BUTTER
4 CUPS CELERY IN 1/2-INCH SLICES
1 TABLESPOON MINCED ONION
1/2 TEASPOON SUGAR
1 CHICKEN BOUILLON CUBE
1/8 TEASPOON POWDERED GINGER OR 1 TEASPOON CHOPPED FRESH OR CRYSTALLIZED GINGER

1. SAUTÉ ALMONDS IN BUTTER UNTIL GOLDEN.

2. ADD CELERY, ONION, SUGAR, CRUSHED BOUILLON CUBE, AND GINGER. COVER AND COOK ABOUT 10 MINUTES, STIRRING OFTEN. ADD DASH OF WHITE PEPPER TO TASTE, IF DESIRED.

YIELD: 4 SERVINGS

GLAZED SLICED CARROTS [M]

8 FRESH CARROTS
1/2 CUP BROWN SUGAR
DASH NUTMEG
3 TABLESPOONS BUTTER

1. DROP SLICED, PEELED CARROTS INTO BOILING WATER AND BLANCH. CARROTS SHOULD REMAIN FAIRLY FIRM.

2. IN LARGE SKILLET OR FLAT MICROWAVE-SAFE DISH, ADD PRECOOKED CARROTS, SUGAR, NUTMEG, AND BUTTER. TO GLAZE, HEAT OVER MEDIUM-HIGH HEAT ON STOVE OR AT 50% POWER IN MICROWAVE, UNTIL SUGAR IS DISSOLVED AND CARROTS ARE GLAZED. SERVE GARNISHED WITH FRESH PARSLEY. *GOES GREAT WITH HAM!*

YIELD: 4 SERVINGS

O IS FOR ONION! [M]

4 ONIONS (3- TO 4-INCH DIAMETER)—VIDALIA, SPANISH, ETC.

1/4 CUP BUTTER   1/2 TEASPOON PAPRIKA

SALT AND PEPPER TO TASTE

1. PEEL. CUT ENDS FROM EACH ONION SO THEY WILL BE LEVEL WHEN PLACED IN A MICROWAVE-SAFE DISH. REMOVE ABOUT 1/2 INCH OF CORE FROM ONE END (USING SPOON OR GRAPEFRUIT SPOON TO REMOVE CORE MAKES THIS PROCESS EASIER).

2. PRESS 1 TABLESPOON BUTTER INTO CORED CENTER OF EACH ONION. SPRINKLE PAPRIKA OVER TOP. ARRANGE IN CIRCLE IN 9-INCH GLASS DISH. COVER WITH PLASTIC WRAP AND MAKE A SMALL SLIT IN ONE CORNER.

3. COOK ON HIGH 12 TO 14 MINUTES OR UNTIL TENDER. LET STAND 5 MINUTES. SALT AND PEPPER BEFORE SERVING.

YIELD: 4 SERVINGS

TOMATO ZUCCHINI SAUTÉ

1 POUND ZUCCHINI, SLICED OR CUBED

1/4 CUP CHOPPED ONION 2 MEDIUM CHOPPED TOMATOES

1 CLOVE GARLIC, MINCED 1/4 TEASPOON OREGANO LEAVES

2 TABLESPOONS OLIVE OIL 1/4 TEASPOON BLACK PEPPER

1/4 CUP SLICED BLACK OLIVES (OPTIONAL)

1/2 CUP GRATED PARMESAN CHEESE (OPTIONAL)

1. SAUTÉ ZUCCHINI, CHOPPED ONION, AND GARLIC IN OLIVE OIL FOR TWO TO THREE MINUTES, OR UNTIL ZUCCHINI IS JUST TENDER.

2. ADD CHOPPED TOMATOES, OREGANO LEAVES, AND BLACK PEPPER. SAUTÉ 5 ADDITIONAL MINUTES.

3. GARNISH WITH OLIVES AND PARMESAN CHEESE, IF DESIRED.

YIELD: 4 TO 6 SERVINGS

A SUGGESTION: SERVE IN INDIVIDUAL RAMEKINS, SPRINKLE WITH CHEESE, AND PLACE UNDER BROILER JUST UNTIL CHEESE MELTS.

RATATOUILLE

1 LARGE EGGPLANT
SALT
1 LARGE ZUCCHINI
2 GREEN PEPPERS
1 LARGE ONION

16-OUNCE CAN TOMATOES
1/3 CUP OLIVE OIL
1 TO 2 LARGE CLOVES GARLIC, MINCED
1 TABLESPOON FRESH BASIL
1 TEASPOON FRESH THYME

SALT AND PEPPER, TO TASTE
1/2 CUP GREEN OR BLACK PITTED OLIVES, SLICED

1. PARE AND CUT EGGPLANT INTO 1-INCH CUBES. SALT HEAVILY AND ALLOW TO SIT IN A COLANDER AT LEAST 30 MINUTES TO DRAW OUT MOISTURE.

2. CUT ZUCCHINI AND GREEN PEPPERS INTO 1/2-INCH CUBES. COARSELY CHOP ONION AND SET ASIDE. DRAIN TOMATOES AND COARSELY CHOP.

3. RINSE EGGPLANT CUBES AND PAT DRY WITH PAPER TOWELS.

4. HEAT OLIVE OIL IN LARGE, HEAVY SAUCEPAN OR SKILLET. SAUTÉ ONION UNTIL GOLDEN. ADD GARLIC AND SAUTÉ BRIEFLY. COMBINE EGGPLANT, ZUCCHINI, PEPPERS, AND TOMATOES.

5. ADD BASIL AND THYME. BRING TO A SIMMER, COVER, AND COOK 30 TO 45 MINUTES, UNTIL VEGETABLES ARE TENDER BUT STILL FIRM. REMOVE LID AND BOIL OFF EXCESS LIQUID.

6. SALT AND PEPPER TO TASTE. STIR IN OLIVES. SERVE HOT OR COLD *WITH FRENCH OR ITALIAN BREAD OR GARLIC TOAST.*

YIELD: 4 SERVINGS

ZUCCHINI WITH CHEESE [F]

LASAGNE-STYLE

4 MEDIUM ZUCCHINI

1 MEDIUM ONION, CHOPPED

1 TABLESPOON OIL

15-OUNCE CAN TOMATO SAUCE

1 TEASPOON ITALIAN SEASONING

SALT AND PEPPER TO TASTE

15 OUNCES COTTAGE CHEESE

1 EGG

2 TABLESPOONS FLOUR

8 OUNCES PART-SKIM MOZZARELLA CHEESE, GRATED

1. SET OVEN TO 350°F. OIL AN 8 X 12-INCH BAKING DISH. SLICE ZUCCHINI IN 1/4-INCH-THICK PIECES.

2. SAUTÉ ONION IN OIL UNTIL TRANSPARENT. ADD TOMATO SAUCE AND SEASONINGS. HEAT TO BOILING. SIMMER FOR 5 MINUTES.

3. COMBINE COTTAGE CHEESE AND EGG.

4. COVER BOTTOM OF PAN WITH A FEW TABLESPOONS OF TOMATO SAUCE. ARRANGE HALF OF ZUCCHINI IN BOTTOM OF BAKING DISH. SPRINKLE WITH 1 TABLESPOON FLOUR. TOP WITH COTTAGE CHEESE AND HALF OF THE TOMATO SAUCE. REPEAT LAYERS WITH THE REMAINING ZUCCHINI, FLOUR, AND TOMATO SAUCE. SPRINKLE WITH MOZZARELLA.

5. BAKE FOR 40 TO 50 MINUTES UNTIL ZUCCHINI IS FORK-TENDER. LET STAND 10 MINUTES FOR EASIER CUTTING.

YIELD: 6 SERVINGS

FOR A VEGETARIAN DINNER OR AN ITALIAN NIGHT SIDE DISH, MAKE THIS AHEAD AND REFRIGERATE COVERED. BAKE UNCOVERED.

VEGETARIAN SPAGHETTI [L+]

4 CUPS PARED, DICED EGGPLANT

1 CUP RAW SPAGHETTI, BROKEN 3/4 CUP WATER

1 1/2 CUPS DICED CELERY 2 TEASPOONS WORCESTERSHIRE SAUCE

1/4 CUP MINCED ONIONS 1 SMALL CLOVE GARLIC, MINCED

3/4 CUP CHOPPED GREEN OLIVES 1/4 TEASPOON BASIL

1 8-OUNCE CAN TOMATO SAUCE 1 TABLESPOON CHOPPED PARSLEY

2 TABLESPOONS OLIVE OIL 1/2 CUP GRATED PARMESAN CHEESE

1. SET OVEN TO 350°F. LAYER EGGPLANT, SPAGHETTI, CELERY, ONION, AND OLIVES IN GREASED 2-QUART CASSEROLE.

2. COMBINE TOMATO SAUCE, OLIVE OIL, WATER, WORCESTERSHIRE SAUCE, GARLIC, BASIL, AND PARSLEY. POUR OVER CASSEROLE INGREDIENTS.

3. COVER AND BAKE FOR 1 1/2 HOURS.

4. REMOVE COVER. SPRINKLE WITH PARMESAN CHEESE. PLACE UNDER BROILER JUST UNTIL CHEESE IS MELTED AND BUBBLY.

YIELD: 4 SERVINGS

SERVE WITH CRISPY ITALIAN BREAD.

BREADS

BREADS

TOAST CRISPS

1 LOAF THINLY SLICED WHITE BREAD

1. SET OVEN TO 200-225°F.

2. TRIM CRUSTS OFF BREAD. CUT DIAGONALLY INTO TRIANGLES. THERE WILL BE 4 TRIANGLES PER SLICE.

3. PLACE ON UNGREASED COOKIE SHEET. BAKE UNTIL PIECES ARE DRY AND **CRISP, BUT NOT BROWNED**. STORE IN AIRTIGHT CONTAINER.

YIELD: 4 TRIANGLES PER SLICE

TOAST CRISPS ARE MILD IN FLAVOR AND WON'T DRAW ATTENTION AWAY FROM YOUR CHEESES OR SPREADS.

POPPING GOOD POPOVERS

2 EGGS | 1 CUP FLOUR
1 CUP MILK | 1/2 TEASPOON SALT

1. BREAK EGGS INTO A BOWL. ADD MILK, FLOUR, AND SALT. MIX WELL **WITH A SPOON. BATTER WILL BE A LITTLE LUMPY— DON'T OVERMIX.** FILL 12 **WELL-GREASED** MUFFIN PANS OR 6 POPOVER PANS.

2. PUT IN A COLD OVEN AND BAKE AT 425°F FOR 30 MINUTES OR UNTIL DONE. DONE IS A DEEP GOLDEN BROWN. DO NOT OPEN OVEN DOOR TO PEEK DURING THE FIRST 30 MINUTES!

YIELD: 12 MUFFINS OR 6 POPOVERS

SERVE WITH PLENTY OF BUTTER. POPOVERS COMPLEMENT CHICKEN AND BEEF DISHES.

KITTY'S SCOTTISH OATMEAL SCONES [F]

1 1/2 CUPS SIFTED FLOUR
1 TABLESPOON BAKING POWDER
1/2 TEASPOON SALT
2 TABLESPOONS SUGAR
1/4 TEASPOON NUTMEG

1/2 TEASPOON GRATED LEMON RIND
1/3 CUP COLD BUTTER
1/2 CUP ROLLED OATS
3/4 CUP RAISINS (OPTIONAL)
2/3 CUP MILK

1. SET OVEN TO 450°F.

2. SIFT FLOUR, BAKING POWDER, SALT, SUGAR, AND NUTMEG IN FOOD PROCESSOR WORK BOWL. ADD LEMON RIND.

3. CUT BUTTER IN 8 TO 10 PIECES AND ADD TO MIXTURE. PROCESS ON AND OFF UNTIL DRY MIXTURE RESEMBLES COARSE CORNMEAL. TRANSFER TO A LARGE BOWL. STIR IN OATS AND OPTIONAL RAISINS.

4. ADD MILK TO DRY INGREDIENTS, MIXING LIGHTLY WITH FORK UNTIL DOUGH LEAVES SIDES OF BOWL.

5. TURN OUT ON FLOURED BOARD AND KNEAD GENTLY A FEW SECONDS. **HANDLE LIGHTLY.** PAT INTO 2 ROUNDS 3/8-INCH THICK. CUT EACH ROUND INTO 6 TRIANGLES.

6. PLACE ON GREASED BAKING SHEET AND BRUSH WITH MELTED BUTTER. SPRINKLE WITH ADDITIONAL SUGAR. BAKE FOR 12 TO 15 MINUTES.

YIELD: 12 SCONES

A POT OF TEA, MARMALADE, BUTTER, AND HOT SCONES ARE THE PERFECT 4 O'CLOCK PICK-ME-UP.

SO-EASY BREAD [F, L]

1 CUP PLUS 2 TABLESPOONS WARM WATER (105-115°F)

1 PACKAGE ACTIVE DRY YEAST	1/4 CUP INSTANT NONFAT DRY MILK
1 TEASPOON SUGAR	1 TEASPOON SALT
2 TABLESPOONS VEGETABLE OIL	OIL AND CORNMEAL
3 CUPS FLOUR	1 EGG WHITE

1. STIR YEAST AND SUGAR INTO WATER. LET STAND UNTIL FOAMY, ABOUT 5 MINUTES.

2. FIT METAL BLADE IN FOOD PROCESSOR. POUR IN OIL AND DRY INGREDIENTS. TURN MACHINE ON AND SLOWLY ADD YEAST MIXTURE THROUGH TUBE. MIX UNTIL DOUGH CLEANS SIDES OF BOWL. IF DOUGH IS DRY AND CRUMBLY, ADD MORE WATER BY THE TEASPOON, WORKING IT IN BEFORE ADDING MORE. IF DOUGH IS TOO STICKY, ADD ADDITIONAL FLOUR A TABLESPOON AT A TIME, MIXING THOROUGHLY AFTER EACH ADDITION.

3. ONCE DESIRED CONSISTENCY IS ACHIEVED (MOIST BUT NOT STICKY), MIX DOUGH UNTIL WELL KNEADED, UNIFORMLY SUPPLE, AND ELASTIC, ABOUT 40 SECONDS IN FOOD PROCESSOR.

4. GREASE ANOTHER BOWL THOROUGHLY AND TRANSFER DOUGH. COVER LOOSELY WITH PLASTIC WRAP OR DISH TOWEL. LET RISE IN WARM SPOT UNTIL DOUBLED, ABOUT 1 TO 1 1/2 HOURS.

5. OIL A 9-INCH LOAF PAN AND DUST WITH CORNMEAL. PUNCH DOUGH DOWN AND SHAPE TO FIT PAN OR TRY A VARIATION.* COVER LOOSELY WITH PLASTIC WRAP OR DISH TOWEL. LET RISE IN WARM SPOT UNTIL DOUBLED, ABOUT 1 HOUR.

(CONTINUED ON NEXT PAGE)

SO-EASY BREAD [F, L] *(CONTINUED)*

6. BEFORE BAKING, PUT RACK IN CENTER OF OVEN. SET OVEN TO 350-375°F. WHEN DOUGH HAS DOUBLED, BRUSH TOP WITH EGG WHITE. IF THE YOLK ACCIDENTALLY BREAKS AND MIXES WITH THE WHITE, DON'T PANIC. THE WHOLE EGG CAN BE USED SUCCESSFULLY TO COAT THE TOP OF THE DOUGH. AT THIS POINT, IF YOU WISH, YOU MAY SPRINKLE LOAF WITH POPPY OR SESAME SEEDS. BAKE UNTIL LOAF IS GOLDEN AND SOUNDS HOLLOW WHEN RAPPED ON BOTTOM, ABOUT 35 MINUTES. IMMEDIATELY REMOVE LOAF FROM PAN TO COOL ON WIRE RACK.

YIELD: 1 LOAF

*VARIATIONS:

PAT OR ROLL DOUGH ON A FLOURED DISH TOWEL TO AN APPROXIMATELY 9 X 16-INCH RECTANGLE. BRUSH LIGHTLY WITH MELTED BUTTER.

THEN

A) SPRINKLE WITH 1/4 CUP FINELY CHOPPED NUTS MIXED WITH 2 TABLESPOONS BROWN SUGAR FOR **NUT BREAD.**

B) SPRINKLE WITH 2 TABLESPOONS SUGAR AND 1/2 TEASPOON CINNAMON FOR **CINNAMON BREAD.**

C) THERE ARE LOADS OF POSSIBILITIES. FOR EXAMPLE, **PIZZA BREAD:** SPRINKLE WITH MINCED PEPPERONI AND SHREDDED MOZZARELLA CHEESE. YUM!

FINALLY

ROLL UP DOUGH JELLY ROLL–FASHION STARTING AT THE 9-INCH SIDE. PINCH ENDS, LAY SEAM-SIDE DOWN IN THE PREPARED PAN. COVER LOOSELY AND LET RISE IN WARM SPOT UNTIL DOUBLED. CONTINUE WITH STEP 6.

RAISIN CINNAMON OATMEAL MUFFINS [F]

1 CUP FLOUR

1/4 CUP SUGAR

3 TEASPOONS BAKING POWDER

1/2 TEASPOON SALT

3 TABLESPOONS COLD BUTTER

1 CUP ROLLED OATS

1/2 CUP SEEDLESS RAISINS

1 BEATEN EGG

1 CUP MILK

1/2 TEASPOON CINNAMON

1 TABLESPOON SUGAR

1. SET OVEN TO 425°F. SIFT TOGETHER FLOUR, 1/4 CUP SUGAR, BAKING POWDER, AND SALT INTO FOOD PROCESSOR BOWL.

2. CUT BUTTER INTO 6 OR 8 PIECES AND ADD TO DRY INGREDIENTS. PULSE FOOD PROCESSOR UNTIL FLOUR/BUTTER MIXTURE RESEMBLES COARSE CORNMEAL, MAYBE 4 OR 5 TIMES. TRANSFER FOOD PROCESSOR CONTENTS TO A BOWL.

3. STIR IN ROLLED OATS AND RAISINS.

4. COMBINE EGG AND MILK. ADD TO DRY INGREDIENTS AND MIX JUST ENOUGH TO DAMPEN.

5. FILL WELL-GREASED MUFFIN PANS TWO-THIRDS FULL. COMBINE CINNAMON WITH 1 TABLESPOON SUGAR. SPRINKLE OVER MUFFINS.

6. BAKE FOR 15 TO 20 MINUTES.

YIELD: 12 MUFFINS

IF YOU WISH TO KEEP MUFFIN MIX ON HAND, CONTINUE THROUGH STEP 3 AND FREEZE. WHEN READY TO USE, DEFROST AND CONTINUE WITH STEP 4. THIS WILL KEEP IN THE FREEZER FOR ABOUT A MONTH.

HAWAIIAN-STYLE RAISIN CARROT MUFFINS

2 CUPS FLOUR

3/4 CUP SUGAR

2 TEASPOONS BAKING POWDER

1/2 TEASPOON GROUND CINNAMON

1/4 TEASPOON GROUND GINGER

1/2 CUP SHREDDED CARROTS

1/2 CUP RAISINS

1/2 CUP CHOPPED NUTS

8-OUNCE CAN CRUSHED PINEAPPLE

2 EGGS

1/2 CUP BUTTER, MELTED

1 TEASPOON VANILLA

1. SET OVEN TO 375°F. SIFT TOGETHER FLOUR, SUGAR, BAKING POWDER, CINNAMON, AND GINGER.

2. STIR IN CARROTS, RAISINS, AND NUTS. SEPARATELY COMBINE **UNDRAINED** PINEAPPLE, EGGS, BUTTER, AND VANILLA. STIR INTO DRY INGREDIENTS UNTIL **JUST BLENDED**.

3. SPOON INTO GREASED MUFFIN TINS OR PAPER-LINED MUFFIN CUPS. BAKE FOR 20 TO 30 MINUTES, DEPENDING ON SIZE OF MUFFINS. TURN OUT ONTO RACK TO COOL.

YIELD: 12 LARGE OR 36 MINI MUFFINS

WE PREFER THE MINI MUFFINS ... THEY'RE LITTLE JEWELS!

VERMONT BROWN BREAD

1 1/2 CUPS WHITE FLOUR
1 CUP WHOLE WHEAT FLOUR
1 1/2 TEASPOONS BAKING SODA
1/2 TEASPOON SALT

1/4 CUP IRISH OATMEAL
1/4 CUP WHEAT GERM
2 TABLESPOONS MOLASSES
2 CUPS BUTTERMILK

1. SET OVEN TO 400°F. GREASE AND FLOUR A LOAF PAN.

2. SIFT TOGETHER WHITE AND WHOLE WHEAT FLOURS, BAKING SODA, AND SALT.

3. STIR IN IRISH OATMEAL AND WHEAT GERM.

4. COMBINE MOLASSES AND BUTTERMILK. ADD TO DRY INGREDIENTS. STIR JUST UNTIL BLENDED.

5. POUR INTO PREPARED PAN. BAKE FOR 40 TO 45 MINUTES OR UNTIL NICELY BROWNED. BREAD IS DONE WHEN LOAF SOUNDS HOLLOW WHEN RAPPED ON BOTTOM.

YIELD: 1 LOAF

IRISH OATMEAL IS QUITE A BIT DIFFERENT FROM AMERICAN ROLLED OATS. THESE ARE WHOLE KERNELS OF OATS THAT GIVE BREAD A DEFINITE TEXTURE. IT CAN BE PURCHASED IN MOST LOCAL IRISH SHOPS. WE TASTED THIS BREAD IN VERMONT AND IT REMINDED US OF THE BREAKFASTS WE HAD WHEN VISITING IRELAND.

CAPE COD COUNTRY INN LEMON LOAF BREAD [X]

6 TABLESPOONS SOFT BUTTER
1 CUP SUGAR
GRATED RIND OF 1 LEMON
2 EGGS, BEATEN

1 1/2 CUPS FLOUR
1 TEASPOON BAKING POWDER
1/4 TEASPOON SALT
1/2 CUP MILK

GLAZE

JUICE OF ONE LEMON

1/2 CUP GRANULATED SUGAR

1. SET OVEN TO 350°F.

2. IN LARGE BOWL, CREAM BUTTER AND SUGAR, ADDING SUGAR GRADUALLY. ADD LEMON RIND AND EGGS. BEAT UNTIL LIGHT.

3. SIFT TOGETHER FLOUR, BAKING POWDER, AND SALT.

4. ADD DRY INGREDIENTS ALTERNATELY WITH MILK, BEATING AFTER EACH ADDITION.

5. SPREAD INTO WELL-GREASED AND FLOURED LOAF PAN. BAKE FOR 50 MINUTES.

6. MIX TOGETHER LEMON JUICE AND SUGAR. POKE HOLES IN CAKE WITH A CAKE TESTER. COVER LOAF WITH GLAZE AND CONTINUE BAKING FOR AN ADDITIONAL 10 MINUTES. COOL COMPLETELY IN PAN. SLICES WELL WHEN CHILLED.

YIELD: 1 LOAF

*WHILE YOU'RE AT IT, MAKE TWO LOAVES AND FREEZE ONE FOR A PARTY NEXT WEEK. **CAPE COD COUNTRY INN LEMON LOAF** IS GREAT FOR A TEA OR FOR A SALAD LUNCHEON IN SUMMER.*

CHOCOLATE RAISIN-NUT TEA BREAD [X]

1/4 CUP SOFT BUTTER
2/3 CUP SUGAR
1 EGG
2 CUPS FLOUR
1 TEASPOON BAKING SODA

1/2 TEASPOON SALT
1/3 CUP COCOA
1/2 TEASPOON CINNAMON
1 CUP BUTTERMILK
1 CUP RAISINS

3/4 CUP CHOPPED NUTS

1. SET OVEN TO 350°F. GREASE AND FLOUR A 9 X 5-INCH LOAF PAN.

2. CREAM BUTTER AND SUGAR, ADDING SUGAR GRADUALLY. ADD EGG AND BEAT WELL.

3. SIFT TOGETHER FLOUR, BAKING SODA, SALT, COCOA, AND CINNAMON. ADD TO CREAMED MIXTURE ALTERNATELY WITH BUTTERMILK, BEATING AFTER EACH ADDITION AND ENDING WITH BUTTERMILK.

4. STIR IN RAISINS AND NUTS.

5. TURN INTO LOAF PAN. BAKE FOR 1 HOUR OR UNTIL DONE. COOL ON WIRE RACK.

YIELD: 1 LOAF

SERVE WITH SOFTENED CREAM CHEESE, IF DESIRED.

PUMPKIN-NUT BREAD [x]

2 CUPS FLOUR

2 TEASPOONS BAKING POWDER

1/2 TEASPOON BAKING SODA

1 TEASPOON SALT

1 TEASPOON CINNAMON

1/2 TEASPOON NUTMEG

1 CUP SUGAR

1 CUP CANNED PUMPKIN

1/2 CUP MILK

2 EGGS

1 TEASPOON VANILLA

1/4 CUP SOFT BUTTER

1 CUP CHOPPED NUTS

1. SET OVEN TO 350°F. SIFT TOGETHER FLOUR, BAKING POWDER, BAKING SODA, SALT, CINNAMON, NUTMEG, AND SUGAR.

2. COMBINE PUMPKIN, MILK, EGGS, AND VANILLA IN MIXING BOWL. ADD SIFTED INGREDIENTS AND BUTTER, **MIXING ONLY UNTIL FLOUR IS MOISTENED.** STIR IN NUTS.

3. TURN INTO WELL-GREASED 9 X 5-INCH LOAF PAN. BAKE FOR 65 MINUTES OR UNTIL WOODEN PICK INSERTED IN CENTER COMES OUT CLEAN. COOL 10 MINUTES. REMOVE FROM PAN.

YIELD: 1 LOAF

ORANGE-RAISIN TEA BREAD [X]

JUICE, GRATED RIND OF 1 LARGE ORANGE

2 TABLESPOONS BUTTER

1 CUP RAISINS

1 BEATEN EGG

1 CUP SUGAR

1 TEASPOON VANILLA

2 CUPS FLOUR

1 TEASPOON BAKING POWDER

1/2 TEASPOON BAKING SODA

1/2 TEASPOON SALT

1. SET OVEN TO 350°F. THOROUGHLY GREASE AND FLOUR A LOAF PAN.

2. MIX JUICE WITH ENOUGH BOILING WATER TO MAKE 1 CUP. PUT IN MIXING BOWL AND ADD BUTTER. WHEN BUTTER IS MELTED, STIR IN ORANGE RIND, RAISINS, EGG, SUGAR, AND VANILLA.

3. SIFT FLOUR, BAKING POWDER, BAKING SODA, AND SALT INTO ABOVE MIXTURE. BLEND AND POUR INTO LOAF PAN. BAKE FOR 1 HOUR.

YIELD: 1 LOAF

SEE HINT ON PAGE 108 FOR JUICING ORANGE AND GRATING RIND.

FRESH CRANBERRY BREAD

2 CUPS FLOUR

1 CUP SUGAR

1 1/2 TEASPOONS BAKING POWDER

1/2 TEASPOON BAKING SODA

1/2 TEASPOON SALT

JUICE, GRATED RIND OF 1 ORANGE

2 TABLESPOONS BUTTER

BOILING WATER

1 EGG, WELL BEATEN

1 CUP CHOPPED NUTS

1 CUP CHOPPED FRESH CRANBERRIES

1. SET OVEN TO 350°F. SIFT TOGETHER FLOUR, SUGAR, BAKING POWDER, BAKING SODA, AND SALT.

2. COMBINE JUICE AND GRATED RIND OF ORANGE WITH BUTTER AND ENOUGH BOILING WATER TO TOTAL 3/4 CUP. ADD EGG.

3. BLEND LIQUIDS INTO DRY INGREDIENTS AND **STIR ONLY UNTIL FLOUR MIXTURE IS DAMPENED.** ADD CHOPPED NUTS AND CRANBERRIES. POUR INTO GREASED 9 X 5 X 3-INCH PAN. BAKE FOR 1 HOUR.

YIELD: 1 LOAF

APRICOT NUT LOAF [X]

---

1 CUP SUGAR

2 TABLESPOONS SOFT BUTTER

1 EGG

3/4 CUP MILK

3/4 CUP ORANGE JUICE

4 TEASPOONS GRATED ORANGE RIND

3 CUPS SIFTED FLOUR

3 1/2 TEASPOONS BAKING POWDER

1 TEASPOON SALT

3/4 CUP CHOPPED NUTS

1 CUP FINELY CHOPPED DRIED APRICOTS

1. SET OVEN TO 350°F. GREASE AND FLOUR A 9 X 5-INCH LOAF PAN.

2. CREAM SUGAR AND BUTTER UNTIL LIGHT AND FLUFFY. ADD EGG AND MIX THOROUGHLY. STIR IN MILK, ORANGE JUICE, AND RIND.

3. SIFT TOGETHER FLOUR, BAKING POWDER, AND SALT. BLEND INTO CREAMED MIXTURE. GENTLY STIR IN NUTS AND APRICOTS.

4. POUR INTO PREPARED PAN. LET STAND FOR 20 MINUTES. BAKE ABOUT 70 MINUTES OR UNTIL TOOTHPICK COMES OUT CLEAN.

YIELD: 1 LOAF

DESSERTS
PIES
PASTRY

DESSERTS • PIES • PASTRY

HINTS:

TO GET EVERY BIT OF JUICE FROM A LEMON OR ORANGE, RUN IT IN THE MICROWAVE FOR ABOUT 20 TO 30 SECONDS OR UNTIL SLIGHTLY WARM TO THE TOUCH. ROLL ON COUNTERTOP. CUT IN HALF AND PLACE IN JUICER. AFTER JUICING, IF YOU NEED GRATED RIND, PUT RINDS IN FREEZER FOR 20 TO 30 MINUTES. WHEN SLIGHTLY FROZEN, THEY ARE MUCH EASIER TO GRATE. WE KEEP EXTRA GRATED LEMON RIND IN THE FREEZER FOR THOSE RECIPES THAT REQUIRE ONLY THE RIND, SUCH AS **KITTY'S SCOTTISH OATMEAL SCONES** AND **LEMON CRUMB TOPPING.**

LEMONY LEMON BARS [x]

CRUST

2 CUPS FLOUR

1 CUP **VERY SOFT** BUTTER

1/2 CUP CONFECTIONERS' SUGAR

TOPPING

4 BEATEN EGGS

1/2 TEASPOON BAKING POWDER

2 CUPS GRANULATED SUGAR

6 TEASPOONS LEMON JUICE

4 TABLESPOONS FLOUR

1 TEASPOON LEMON RIND

ADDITIONAL CONFECTIONERS' SUGAR

1. SET OVEN TO 350°F.

2. IN BOWL, MIX FLOUR, BUTTER, AND CONFECTIONERS' SUGAR WITH FINGERS. PAT INTO A 9 X 13-INCH PAN AND BAKE FOR 15 TO 20 MINUTES. SET ASIDE UNTIL TOPPING IS PREPARED.

3. BEAT EGGS, SUGAR, FLOUR, BAKING POWDER, LEMON JUICE, AND LEMON RIND TOGETHER. POUR OVER BAKED CRUST. BAKE FOR ADDITIONAL 25 MINUTES OR UNTIL NO IMPRINT REMAINS WHEN LIGHTLY TOUCHED IN CENTER.

4. SPRINKLE WITH CONFECTIONERS' SUGAR WHILE STILL HOT. CUT INTO 2-INCH SQUARES WHEN COOL. SERVE AT ROOM TEMPERATURE.

YIELD: 24 TO 30 BARS

*THESE **LEMONY LEMON BARS** HAVE A LEMON MERINGUE PIE FLAVOR WITHOUT ALL THE FUSS. REFRIGERATE ANY LEFTOVERS.*

CRANBERRY CRUNCH [X]

1/2 CUP SOFT BUTTER   1/2 CUP FLOUR

1 CUP LIGHT BROWN SUGAR   1 CUP ROLLED OATS

1/2 TEASPOON CINNAMON   1 POUND CAN WHOLE CRANBERRY SAUCE

1 QUART VANILLA ICE CREAM

1. PREHEAT OVEN TO 350°F.

2. IN MIXING BOWL, CREAM BUTTER, SUGAR, AND CINNAMON.

3. STIR FLOUR AND OATS INTO CREAMED MIXTURE WITH FORK (MIXTURE WILL BE CRUMBLY).

4. SPREAD HALF OF MIXTURE OVER BOTTOM OF GREASED 8 X 8-INCH BAKING DISH. BREAK UP CRANBERRY SAUCE WITH A FORK. COVER CRUMBS WITH CRANBERRY SAUCE. TOP WITH REMAINING CRUMBS.

5. BAKE FOR 45 MINUTES. SERVE HOT OR WARM IN SQUARES TOPPED WITH SCOOPS OF VANILLA ICE CREAM.

YIELD: 9 SERVINGS

THIS CRUNCH ALSO COULD BE MADE WITH GOOD RESULTS BY USING ANY CAN OF FRUIT PIE FILLING.

SPICY IRISH APPLE CRISP [F, X]

---

6 LARGE CRISP APPLES (E.G. STAYMAN OR WINESAP)

1/2 CUP WATER   1/2 CUP GRANULATED SUGAR

1/2 TEASPOON EACH CINNAMON, NUTMEG, AND GINGER

1/8 TEASPOON EACH GROUND CLOVES AND SALT

1/2 CUP BROWN SUGAR   1/2 CUP QUICK-COOKING OATS

1/2 CUP COLD BUTTER   3/4 CUP FLOUR

1. SET OVEN TO 350°F.

2. PEEL APPLES, CUT IN QUARTERS, AND REMOVE CORE. STAND APPLES ON END IN THE TUBE OF THE FOOD PROCESSOR AND SLICE THIN.

3. PLACE APPLES IN GREASED 8-INCH SQUARE PAN. SPRINKLE WITH WATER.

4. COMBINE GRANULATED SUGAR, CINNAMON, NUTMEG, GINGER, CLOVES, AND SALT. SPRINKLE OVER APPLES.

5. BEAT BROWN SUGAR AND BUTTER. WITH FORK, STIR OATS AND FLOUR INTO BROWN SUGAR/BUTTER MIXTURE. SPRINKLE OVER APPLES.

6. BAKE FOR 30 MINUTES OR UNTIL APPLES ARE TENDER.

YIELD: 6 SERVINGS

POTS DE CREME AU CHOCOLAT [B, M]

8 OUNCES SEMISWEET CHOCOLATE CHIPS
1 1/4 CUPS LIGHT CREAM   1 TEASPOON VANILLA
1 EGG   1 TABLESPOON COINTREAU

1. IN MICROWAVE, MELT CHOCOLATE. ADD CREAM AND HEAT UNTIL NEARLY BOILING.

2. POUR HEATED CREAM/CHOCOLATE MIXTURE INTO BLENDER AND PULSE UNTIL JUST BLENDED. ADD EGG; BLEND AT HIGH SPEED FOR 2 MINUTES. THEN ADD VANILLA AND COINTREAU TO INGREDIENTS. CONTINUE PROCESSING IN BLENDER FOR AN ADDITIONAL 2 MINUTES AT HIGH SPEED.

3. POUR INTO INDIVIDUAL DESSERT GLASSES. CHILL **AT LEAST 12 HOURS**. SERVE TOPPED WITH FRESH WHIPPED CREAM.

YIELD: 6 4-OUNCE SERVINGS

*JUST ADD 1/2 TEASPOON INSTANT COFFEE AND SUBSTITUTE 1 TABLESPOON KAHLUA FOR COINTREAU TO CREATE **POTS DE CREME AU MOCHA**.*

APRICOT STRUDEL

1/2 CUP BUTTER

1 CUP FLOUR

1/4 TEASPOON SALT

1/2 CUP DAIRY SOUR CREAM

3/4 CUP APRICOT PRESERVES

1/2 CUP FLAKED COCONUT

1/3 CUP CHOPPED PECANS

1. CUT BUTTER INTO FLOUR AND SALT UNTIL CRUMBLY. THEN MIX IN SOUR CREAM. COVER AND REFRIGERATE OVERNIGHT.

2. TAKE FROM REFRIGERATOR THE NEXT DAY AND LET STAND UNTIL DOUGH IS AT ROOM TEMPERATURE. ROLL OUT INTO A RECTANGLE 10 X 15 INCHES, USING ONLY ENOUGH FLOUR TO KEEP DOUGH FROM STICKING.

3. SET OVEN TO 350°F. SPREAD DOUGH WITH APRICOT PRESERVES. SPRINKLE ON COCONUT AND PECANS.

4. ROLL UP LIKE A JELLY ROLL, BEGINNING WITH THE LONG SIDE. THE FINISHED ROLL IS 15 INCHES LONG.

5. PLACE ON A WELL-GREASED BAKING SHEET. BAKE FOR 1 HOUR.

6. REMOVE FROM OVEN. LET STAND 10 MINUTES, THEN CUT WITH A SHARP KNIFE INTO DESIRED SIZED PIECES. CUTTING IT INTO 9 PIECES MAKES NICE-SIZED DESSERT SERVINGS. SPRINKLE WITH CONFECTIONERS' SUGAR. FOR BEST FLAVOR, SERVE WARM.

YIELD: APPROXIMATELY 9 SERVINGS

PEACH CREAM PIE

UNBAKED PIE SHELL

2 TEASPOONS FLOUR

4 CUPS PEELED, SLICED, FRESH PEACHES

1/2 CUP SUGAR

1/2 TEASPOON CINNAMON

1 EGG

2 TABLESPOONS CREAM

1. SET OVEN TO 400°F.

2. PUT PIE SHELL IN OVEN FOR 5 MINUTES TO SET. REMOVE AND SPRINKLE BOTTOM OF SHELL WITH FLOUR.

3. ARRANGE PEACHES IN PIE SHELL. MIX SUGAR AND CINNAMON AND SPRINKLE OVER PEACHES. **IF PEACHES ARE EXTRA-SWEET, REDUCE SUGAR TO 1/3 CUP.** BEAT EGG AND CREAM. POUR OVER PEACHES.

4. SPRINKLE **LEMON CRUMB TOPPING** (SEE BELOW) OVER TOP OF PIE.

5. BAKE UNTIL LIGHTLY BROWNED, APPROXIMATELY 40 TO 45 MINUTES.

YIELD: 1 PIE

LEMON CRUMB TOPPING [X]

1/4 CUP LIGHT BROWN SUGAR

1/4 CUP SOFT BUTTER

1 TEASPOON GRATED LEMON PEEL

1/2 CUP FLOUR

1. BEAT TOGETHER SUGAR, BUTTER, AND LEMON PEEL.

2. WITH FORK, STIR IN FLOUR. SPRINKLE ON PIE.

ROCHESTER AUDUBON PIE [X]

1/3 CUP BUTTER

1 CUP SUGAR (RESERVE 2 TABLESPOONS TO SPRINKLE ON TOP OF PIE)

1 EGG   1 CUP FLOUR

1/2 TEASPOON EACH CINNAMON, NUTMEG, AND GINGER

1/8 TEASPOON EACH SALT AND GROUND CLOVES

1 TEASPOON BAKING SODA   2 1/2 TO 3 CUPS CHOPPED APPLES

1/2 CUP CHOPPED NUTS

1. SET OVEN TO 350°F. BUTTER A 9-INCH PIE PAN.

2. IN A LARGE MIXING BOWL, CREAM BUTTER AND SUGAR TOGETHER. ADD EGG AND BEAT UNTIL LIGHT AND FLUFFY.

3. SIFT FLOUR, CINNAMON, NUTMEG, GINGER, SALT, CLOVES, AND BAKING SODA INTO MIXING BOWL. BEAT IN THOROUGHLY.

4. GENTLY STIR APPLES AND NUTS INTO BATTER.

5. PILE INTO PIE PAN AND SPRINKLE TOP WITH RESERVED 2 TABLESPOONS SUGAR.

6. BAKE FOR 30 TO 35 MINUTES OR UNTIL DONE.

YIELD: 1 9-INCH PIE

SERVE EITHER WARM OR COLD WITH ICE CREAM, WHIPPED CREAM, OR SOUR CREAM. SUGGESTION: MAKE THESE IN PAPER-LINED CUPCAKE TINS FOR COFFEE BREAKS, LUNCH BOXES, ETC. MAKES 12 CUPCAKES.

LEMON CAKE PIE [X]

1 LEMON, JUICE AND GRATED PEEL
9-INCH UNBAKED PIE SHELL
2 EGGS, SEPARATED
1 CUP SUGAR

1/4 CUP FLOUR
1/4 CUP BUTTER
1/4 TEASPOON SALT
1 CUP MILK

1. SET OVEN TO 350°F. PRICK BOTTOM OF PIE SHELL WITH A FORK. BAKE PIE SHELL FOR 10 MINUTES.

2. IN SMALL MIXER BOWL, BEAT EGG WHITES UNTIL STIFF, BUT NOT DRY. SET ASIDE.

3. IN LARGE MIXER BOWL, COMBINE SUGAR, FLOUR, BUTTER, SALT, AND EGG YOLKS. BEAT UNTIL SMOOTH. ADD MILK, LEMON JUICE, AND RIND, BEATING SLOWLY. FOLD IN BEATEN EGG WHITES.

4. POUR FILLING IN PIE SHELL. BAKE 40 MINUTES OR UNTIL FILLING IS FIRM. WHEN CUT, THERE WILL BE A DELICATE CAKE ON TOP OF THE PIE FILLING.

YIELD: 1 9-INCH PIE

HERE'S WHERE YOUR EGG SEPARATOR COMES IN VERY HANDY! **LEMON CAKE PIE** *WOULD MAKE A GREAT FINALE FOR MOST FISH ENTRÉES.*

CAPE COD APPLE PIE

UNBAKED PIE SHELL
2 CUPS CHOPPED, PEELED APPLES   1/4 CUP SUGAR
1 LARGE CAN WHOLE CRANBERRY SAUCE   1 TEASPOON INSTANT TAPIOCA
CRUMB TOPPING

1. SET OVEN TO 375°F. PREBAKE PIE SHELL FOR ABOUT 5 MINUTES TO SET.

2. IN BOWL STIR APPLES, CRANBERRY SAUCE, SUGAR, AND INSTANT TAPIOCA. SPRINKLE WITH **CRUMB TOPPING**.

3. PUT INTO PIE SHELL AND BAKE FOR 40 MINUTES OR UNTIL PIE BEGINS TO BUBBLE.

YIELD: 1 PIE

FRENCH SILK CHOCOLATE PIE [X]

9-INCH PIE SHELL
3 OUNCES UNSWEETENED CHOCOLATE
3/4 CUP SOFTENED BUTTER
1 1/2 CUPS CONFECTIONERS' SUGAR

1 1/2 TEASPOONS VANILLA
3 EGGS
WHIPPED CREAM
CHOPPED NUTS

1. SET OVEN TO 400°F. PRICK BOTTOM OF PIE SHELL WITH A FORK. BAKE 12 MINUTES OR UNTIL GOLDEN BROWN. SET ASIDE TO COOL.

2. MELT CHOCOLATE AND COOL SLIGHTLY.

3. WITH AN ELECTRIC MIXER, CREAM BUTTER. ADD SUGAR AND MIX UNTIL VERY WELL BLENDED. THE BUTTER/SUGAR COMBINATION SHOULD BE SMOOTH, FLUFFY, AND PALE YELLOW. BEAT IN CHOCOLATE AND VANILLA.

4. **ADD EGGS, ONE AT A TIME, BEATING VERY WELL AFTER EACH ADDITION.**

5. TURN MIXTURE INTO PIE SHELL AND CHILL SEVERAL HOURS. DECORATE WITH WHIPPED CREAM AND CHOPPED NUTS BEFORE SERVING.

YIELD: 1 9-INCH PIE

CRAN-RAISIN THANKSGIVING PIE

2 1/2 CUPS CHOPPED CRANBERRIES

1 1/2 CUPS CHOPPED RAISINS

1 1/3 CUPS SUGAR

3 TABLESPOONS WATER

3 TABLESPOONS QUICK-COOKING TAPIOCA

9-INCH PIE SHELL AND **CRUMB TOPPING**

1. SET OVEN TO 425°F. PLACE PIE SHELL IN OVEN FOR 5 MINUTES TO SET.

2. COMBINE ALL INGREDIENTS. FILL CRUST WITH MIXTURE. SPRINKLE WITH **CRUMB TOPPING**.

3. BAKE FOR 35 TO 40 MINUTES.

YIELD: 1 9-INCH PIE

CRUMB TOPPING [X]

1/2 CUP SOFTENED BUTTER
1/2 CUP WHITE OR BROWN SUGAR
1/4 TEASPOON CINNAMON (OPTIONAL)
1 CUP FLOUR

1. IN MIXING BOWL, BEAT BUTTER AND SUGAR TOGETHER UNTIL LIGHT AND FLUFFY.

2. COMBINE OPTIONAL CINNAMON WITH FLOUR. USING A FORK, **STIR BY HAND** INTO BUTTER MIXTURE.

3. SPRINKLE AS NEEDED AND BAKE.

YIELD: ABOUT 1 CUP

BROWN SUGAR CRUMB CRUSTS ARE VERY GOOD OVER APPLE, PEACH, OR CRANBERRY PIES.

WHITE SUGAR CRUMB CRUSTS ARE BETTER FOR CHERRY, BLUEBERRY, RHUBARB, OR OTHER PIES.

ALL-PURPOSE GRAHAM CRACKER CRUST [F]

1 1/2 CUPS GRAHAM CRACKER CRUMBS   1/2 CUP SOFT BUTTER
1/4 CUP CONFECTIONERS' SUGAR

1. PUT GRAHAM CRACKER CRUMBS INTO FOOD PROCESSOR WORK BOWL. ADD BUTTER AND SUGAR. PULSE ON AND OFF SEVERAL TIMES, THEN PROCESS UNTIL BUTTER IS ABSORBED INTO MIXTURE.

2. PRESS CRUMB MIXTURE FIRMLY AGAINST BOTTOM OF PAN OR BAKING CUPS. IF YOU WISH, SHELL MAY BE PLACED IN OVEN FOR 5 MINUTES AT 350°F TO SET. COOL BEFORE FILLING.

YIELD: 1 10-INCH PIE SHELL OR 12 CUPCAKE-SIZED SHELLS

FOOLPROOF PIE CRUST

4 CUPS FLOUR

1 TABLESPOON SUGAR

2 TEASPOONS SALT

1 3/4 CUPS SHORTENING

1/2 CUP WATER

1 TABLESPOON VINEGAR

1 LARGE EGG

1. STIR FLOUR, SUGAR, AND SALT IN LARGE BOWL. CUT IN SHORTENING WITH PASTRY BLENDER OR TWO KNIVES.

2. IN SMALL BOWL, BEAT TOGETHER WATER, VINEGAR, AND EGG. ADD TO FLOUR MIXTURE AND STIR UNTIL MOISTENED.

3. DIVIDE INTO 5 PORTIONS. WRAP EACH PORTION IN PLASTIC WRAP. CHILL 1/2 HOUR BEFORE ROLLING OUT.

4. THIS CRUST **CAN ALSO BE PRESSED** INTO A PIE PAN WITH FINGERS OR THE BOTTOM OF A GLASS. RECIPE MAKES 5 ROLLED OR 4 "PRESSED" SHELLS.

YIELD: 4 OR 5 PIE SHELLS

THESE SHELLS MAY BE FROZEN, UNBAKED, RIGHT IN THE PIE PAN AND WILL REMAIN FRESH FOR 2 MONTHS.

CAKES
COOKIES
FROSTINGS

CAKES • COOKIES • FROSTINGS

HINTS:

MOST COOKIE DOUGH CAN BE FORMED INTO ROLLS AND CHILLED. CUTTING OFF EQUAL PIECES IS EASIER THAN DROPPING THEM BY SPOONFULS AND MAKES THEM MORE UNIFORM IN SIZE. AFTER BAKING, LET COOKIES SET ON SHEET FOR 5 MINUTES TO MAKE REMOVAL EASIER.

PLAIN CHEESECAKE [X]

1 PREPARED **GRAHAM CRACKER CRUST**
2 8-OUNCE PACKAGES CREAM CHEESE
2 EGGS

1/2 CUP SUGAR
PINCH SALT
1/2 TEASPOON VANILLA

2 TEASPOONS FRESH LEMON JUICE

TOPPING

1 CUP SOUR CREAM
PINCH SALT

2 TABLESPOONS SUGAR
1/2 TEASPOON VANILLA

1. SET OVEN TO 350°F. SOFTEN CREAM CHEESE. BEAT CHEESE, EGGS, AND SUGAR WITH MIXER. ADD REMAINING CHEESECAKE INGREDIENTS.

2. POUR INTO SHELL AND BAKE FOR 20 MINUTES OR UNTIL CENTER IS ALMOST SET. COOL 5 MINUTES BEFORE SPREADING WITH TOPPING.

3. COMBINE ALL TOPPING INGREDIENTS. SPREAD ONTO PIE. BAKE FOR ADDITIONAL 10 MINUTES. COOL AND REFRIGERATE BEFORE SERVING. IF DESIRED, TOP WITH PIE FILLING OR FRESH FRUIT.

YIELD: 8 TO 10 SERVINGS

TO MAKE INDIVIDUAL CHEESECAKES, LINE MUFFIN CUPS WITH PAPER LINERS AND DROP 1 VANILLA WAFER IN THE BOTTOM. FILL CUPS 3/4 FULL WITH CHEESECAKE MIXTURE. BAKE AT 350°F FOR 15 MINUTES. REMOVE FROM OVEN. SPREAD TOPPING MIX ON EACH CUPCAKE. RETURN TO OVEN AND BAKE FOR ANOTHER 5 TO 7 MINUTES.

YIELD: 12 SMALL CHEESECAKES

WALNUT PRALINE CHEESECAKE [X]

1 3/4 POUNDS CREAM CHEESE
1 CUP GRAHAM CRACKER CRUMBS
1/4 CUP BUTTER, SOFTENED
2 TABLESPOONS WHITE SUGAR
1/2 CUP PACKED DARK BROWN SUGAR

2 EGGS, LIGHTLY BEATEN
1 TEASPOON VANILLA
2 TABLESPOONS FLOUR
1/4 CUP WALNUTS, CHOPPED
WHIPPED CREAM

1. SET OVEN TO 350°F. SOFTEN CREAM CHEESE TO ROOM TEMPERATURE. BUTTER 9-INCH SPRINGFORM PAN. COMBINE GRAHAM CRACKER CRUMBS, BUTTER, AND WHITE SUGAR. PRESS MIXTURE ONTO BOTTOM OF PAN. BAKE ON MIDDLE OVEN RACK FOR 10 MINUTES. LET COOL COMPLETELY.

2. CREAM THE CREAM CHEESE IN LARGE BOWL UNTIL SMOOTH, USING MEDIUM SPEED OF ELECTRIC MIXER. ADD BROWN SUGAR AND MIX THOROUGHLY. SLOWLY ADD IN EGGS AND VANILLA, BEATING WELL.

3. SIFT IN FLOUR AND BEAT UNTIL SMOOTH. FOLD IN WALNUTS, USING SPATULA.

4. POUR BATTER EVENLY OVER CRUST. BAKE ABOUT 45 TO 50 MINUTES OR UNTIL GOLDEN BROWN. LET COOL ON RACK 1 1/2 HOURS.

5. REMOVE SPRINGFORM PAN AND CHILL CHEESECAKE IN REFRIGERATOR FOR AT LEAST 2 HOURS. SERVE TOPPED WITH DOLLOP OF WHIPPED CREAM AND WALNUT HALVES, IF DESIRED.

YIELD: 8 TO 10 SERVINGS

SPICY PRUNE WHIP CAKE [x]

2 CUPS FLOUR

1 1/3 CUPS SUGAR

2 TEASPOONS BAKING POWDER

1/4 TEASPOON BAKING SODA

1 TEASPOON SALT

1/2 CUP SOFT BUTTER

1/2 CUP PRUNE JUICE

1/2 CUP MILK

1 TEASPOON VANILLA

2 EGGS

1/2 TEASPOON EACH OF GROUND CINNAMON, NUTMEG, AND ALLSPICE

3/4 CUP WALNUTS OR PECANS

1. SET OVEN TO 350°F. GREASE AND FLOUR 2 8-INCH CAKE PANS.

2. SIFT DRY INGREDIENTS TOGETHER.

3. MIX DRY INGREDIENTS WITH BUTTER, PRUNE JUICE, 1/4 CUP OF THE MILK, AND VANILLA. BEAT WELL. ADD EGGS AND REMAINING MILK. BEAT 2 MINUTES MORE. FOLD IN NUTS.

4. POUR BATTER INTO PANS. BAKE FOR 30 TO 35 MINUTES. COOL 5 MINUTES. REMOVE FROM PANS.

5. WHEN COOL, FROST WITH **CREAM CHEESE FROSTING**.

YIELD: 2 8-INCH LAYERS

CHOCOLATE-CHERRY CORDIAL CAKE [M, X]

1 PACKAGE FUDGE CAKE MIX
1 CAN CHERRY PIE FILLING
2 EGGS, BEATEN
1 TEASPOON ALMOND EXTRACT

1 CUP SUGAR
1/3 CUP MILK
5 TABLESPOONS BUTTER
1 CUP CHOCOLATE MORSELS

1. SET OVEN TO 350°F. GREASE AND FLOUR A 9 X 13-INCH OR BUNDT PAN.

2. MIX FIRST 4 INGREDIENTS TOGETHER, USING LOW SPEED ON MIXER. MIX ONLY UNTIL DRY INGREDIENTS HAVE BEEN MOISTENED. CHERRY PIECES SHOULD BE IN CHUNKS.

3. BAKE FOR 30 TO 40 MINUTES OR IF USING A BUNDT PAN, BAKE FOR 1 HOUR OR UNTIL CAKE TESTS DONE.

4. FOR EASY CHOCOLATE FROSTING, COOK SUGAR, MILK, AND BUTTER IN A SAUCEPAN IN MICROWAVE UNTIL SUGAR IS TOTALLY DISSOLVED. BOIL FOR 1 MINUTE. REMOVE AND ADD CHOCOLATE BITS. RETURN TO MICROWAVE FOR A FEW SECONDS IF CHOCOLATE CHIPS DON'T MELT. BEAT RAPIDLY. POUR OVER CAKE IN PAN.

YIELD: 1 9 X 13-INCH OR BUNDT CAKE

A DUSTING OF CONFECTIONERS' SUGAR MAY BE USED IN PLACE OF TOPPING OR DRIZZLE WITH VANILLA FROSTING.

YOGI'S FAVORITE CHOCOLATE CAKE [X]

2 CUPS SUGAR

2 CUPS FLOUR

3/4 CUP COCOA

2 TEASPOONS BAKING SODA

2 TEASPOONS BAKING POWDER

1/2 TEASPOON SALT

2 EGGS

1/2 CUP COOKING OIL

1 CUP MILK

1 CUP STRONG, BOILING COFFEE

1 1/2 TEASPOONS VANILLA

1. SET OVEN TO 350°F. GREASE AND FLOUR A 9 X 13-INCH PAN OR 2 9-INCH ROUND CAKE PANS.

2. IN A LARGE BOWL, SIFT TOGETHER SUGAR, FLOUR, COCOA, BAKING SODA, BAKING POWDER, AND SALT.

3. BEAT EGGS, OIL, MILK, COFFEE, AND VANILLA AND ADD TO DRY INGREDIENTS. MIXTURE IS VERY THIN.

4. POUR INTO PAN OR PANS. BAKE 40 MINUTES FOR A 9 X 13-INCH CAKE OR APPROXIMATELY 30 MINUTES FOR 2 LAYER CAKES.

YIELD: 1 9 X 13-INCH CAKE OR 2 9-INCH LAYER CAKES

INSTANT AND/OR DECAFFEINATED COFFEE CAN BE USED SUCCESSFULLY IN THIS RECIPE.

FOR THOSE WHO WANT THE TOTAL CHOCOLATE EXPERIENCE, TOP WITH **JAN'S CHOCOLATE LOVER'S FROSTING.**

HAZELNUT RASPBERRY TORTE [F, X]

4 EGGS

3/4 CUP SUGAR

1 TEASPOON VANILLA

1 1/2 CUPS **FINELY** GROUND HAZELNUTS

1 CUP GRAHAM CRACKER CRUMBS

1/2 CUP FLOUR

1/2 CUP SEEDLESS RASPBERRY JAM

1 CUP WHIPPING CREAM

2 TABLESPOONS CONFECTIONERS' SUGAR

1/2 TEASPOON VANILLA

1 CAN CHOCOLATE FROSTING OR **JAN'S CHOCOLATE LOVER'S FROSTING**

1. SET OVEN TO 375°F. GREASE, FLOUR, AND LINE WITH PARCHMENT 2 8-INCH ROUND BAKING PANS. LIGHTLY GREASE PARCHMENT PAPER.

2. BEAT EGGS, SUGAR, AND VANILLA UNTIL ALMOST STIFF. BLEND TOGETHER HAZELNUTS, GRAHAM CRACKER CRUMBS, AND FLOUR. **FOLD** INTO EGG/SUGAR MIXTURE.

3. POUR INTO BAKING PANS. BAKE FOR 15 MINUTES OR UNTIL CENTER IS SET AND CAKE SLIGHTLY PULLS AWAY FROM PAN. **DO NOT OVERBAKE**. COOL.

4. TO MAKE WHIPPED CREAM, COMBINE CREAM, CONFECTIONERS' SUGAR, AND VANILLA. WHIP UNTIL STIFF.

5. PLACE 1 LAYER OF CAKE ON SERVING PLATE. SPREAD WITH CHOCOLATE FROSTING. LET STAND FOR A FEW MINUTES. THEN TOP WITH RASPBERRY JAM. SET ON SECOND LAYER. FROST CAKE WITH CHOCOLATE FROSTING. MAKE WHIPPED CREAM AVAILABLE.

YIELD: 12 TO 16 SERVINGS

RHUBARB COFFEE CAKE [X]

1 CUP GRANULATED SUGAR
1 CUP SOUR CREAM
1 EGG
1 1/2 CUPS FLOUR

1 TEASPOON BAKING SODA
1/2 TEASPOON SALT
2 CUPS CHOPPED RHUBARB
1/2 CUP BROWN SUGAR

1/2 CUP CHOPPED NUTS

1. SET OVEN TO 350°F. GREASE AND FLOUR A 7 X 11-INCH BAKING PAN.

2. BEAT GRANULATED SUGAR, SOUR CREAM, AND EGG.

3. SIFT FLOUR, BAKING SODA, AND SALT INTO SUGAR MIXTURE.

4. STIR IN RHUBARB.

5. POUR IN PREPARED PAN. SPRINKLE WITH A MIXTURE OF BROWN SUGAR AND NUTS. BAKE FOR 30 TO 35 MINUTES. IF USING FROZEN RHUBARB, CAKE MAY BAKE 15 TO 20 MINUTES LONGER.

YIELD: 1 CAKE

THIS MAKES A DISTINCTIVE COFFEE CAKE!

ORANGE-KISSED CAKE [X]

1 1/4 CUPS BOILING WATER
1 CUP QUICK-COOKING OATS
1/2 CUP SOFT BUTTER
1 CUP GRANULATED SUGAR
1/2 CUP PACKED BROWN SUGAR
2 EGGS
1/4 CUP FROZEN ORANGE JUICE

1 TEASPOON VANILLA
1 3/4 CUPS FLOUR
1 TEASPOON BAKING POWDER
1 TEASPOON BAKING SODA
1/2 TEASPOON SALT
1/2 TEASPOON GROUND CINNAMON
1/2 CUP CHOPPED PECANS

1. SET OVEN TO 350°F. GREASE AND FLOUR A 9 X 13-INCH BAKING PAN.

2. POUR BOILING WATER OVER OATS. SET ASIDE.

3. CREAM BUTTER WITH GRANULATED AND BROWN SUGARS. BEAT IN EGGS ONE AT A TIME. BEAT IN ORANGE JUICE CONCENTRATE AND VANILLA.

4. SIFT TOGETHER FLOUR, BAKING POWDER, BAKING SODA, SALT, AND CINNAMON. BLEND INTO CREAMED MIXTURE ALTERNATELY WITH OATS, BEGINNING AND ENDING WITH FLOUR MIXTURE. FOLD IN PECANS.

5. POUR INTO BAKING PAN. BAKE FOR 40 MINUTES OR UNTIL CAKE IS DONE. COOL AND SPREAD WITH **DOUBLE NUT TOPPING**. PLACE UNDER BROILER 1 MINUTE, UNTIL TOPPING IS GOLDEN BROWN AND BUBBLY. SERVE WARM OR COLD.

YIELD: 12 SERVINGS

ORANGE-RAISIN BREAKFAST CAKE [X]

1/2 CUP FROZEN ORANGE JUICE CONCENTRATE, THAWED

2 CUPS FLOUR   1/2 CUP BUTTER

1 CUP SUGAR   1/2 CUP MILK

1 TEASPOON BAKING SODA   2 EGGS

1 TEASPOON SALT   1 CUP RAISINS

1/3 CUP NUTS

1. SET OVEN TO 350°F. GREASE AND FLOUR A 9 X 13-INCH PAN.

2. COMBINE ALL INGREDIENTS TOGETHER. IN MIXER, BLEND AT LOWEST SPEED FOR 30 SECONDS. BEAT 3 MINUTES AT MEDIUM SPEED. POUR INTO PAN.

3. BAKE FOR 40 TO 45 MINUTES. REMOVE CAKE FROM OVEN.

NUT TOPPING:

1/4 CUP FROZEN ORANGE JUICE CONCENTRATE, THAWED

1/3 CUP SUGAR   1/3 CUP CHOPPED NUTS

1 TEASPOON CINNAMON

4. DRIZZLE 1/4 CUP ORANGE JUICE CONCENTRATE OVER HOT CAKE.

5. MIX ALL OTHER INGREDIENTS TOGETHER. SPRINKLE ON CAKE.

YIELD: 1 9 X 13-INCH CAKE

OATMEAL CAKE [X]

1 CUP QUICK-COOKING OATS
1 1/2 CUPS HOT WATER
1/2 CUP BUTTER
1 CUP DARK BROWN SUGAR
1 CUP GRANULATED SUGAR

2 EGGS
1 TEASPOON VANILLA
1 1/3 CUPS FLOUR
1/2 TEASPOON SALT
1 TEASPOON BAKING SODA

1 CUP CHOPPED NUTS

1. SET OVEN TO 350°F. GREASE AND FLOUR A 9 X 13-INCH PAN.

2. COMBINE OATS AND WATER AND SET ASIDE TO COOL.

3. CREAM BUTTER AND SUGARS UNTIL LIGHT AND FLUFFY. BEAT IN EGGS, ONE AT A TIME. ADD VANILLA.

4. SIFT FLOUR, SALT, AND BAKING SODA TOGETHER AND ADD TO CREAMED MIXTURE.

5. GENTLY STIR IN NUTS. FOLD IN THE COOLED OATMEAL AND POUR INTO PREPARED PAN. BAKE FOR 40 MINUTES OR UNTIL CAKE TESTS DONE. TRY **BROILED COCONUT FROSTING** FOR TOPPING.

YIELD: 18 SERVINGS

CHOCOLATE PEANUT CHIP COOKIES [X]

1 1/4 CUPS SOFTENED BUTTER

2 CUPS SUGAR

2 EGGS

2 TEASPOONS VANILLA

2 CUPS FLOUR

3/4 CUP COCOA*

1 TEASPOON BAKING SODA

1/2 TEASPOON SALT

10-OUNCE PACKAGE PEANUT BUTTER CHIPS

1/2 CUP PEANUTS (OPTIONAL)

1. SET OVEN TO 350°F.

2. IN LARGE MIXING BOWL, BEAT BUTTER AND SUGAR UNTIL LIGHT AND FLUFFY. ADD EGGS AND VANILLA; BEAT WELL.

3. STIR TOGETHER FLOUR, COCOA, BAKING SODA, AND SALT. GRADUALLY BLEND INTO BUTTER MIXTURE. STIR IN CHIPS AND OPTIONAL NUTS. CHILL SLIGHTLY.

4. FORM INTO ROLLS 1-INCH IN DIAMETER. CUT INTO 1/2- TO 1-INCH-THICK SLICES. PLACE ON UNGREASED COOKIE SHEET. PUT 15 COOKIES ON EACH SHEET (5 ROWS OF 3 ACROSS). BAKE 8 TO 9 MINUTES. COOKIES WILL BE SOFT; THEY WILL PUFF WHILE BAKING AND FLATTEN WHILE COOLING. COOL SLIGHTLY. REMOVE FROM COOKIE SHEET TO WIRE RACK. COOL COMPLETELY.

YIELD: APPROXIMATELY 7 DOZEN COOKIES

EUROPEAN-STYLE COCOA USED IN PLACE OF TRADITIONAL COCOA MAKES A DARKER CHOCOLATE COOKIE.

ALSO TRY USING CHOCOLATE CHIPS IN PLACE OF PEANUT BUTTER CHIPS OR A COMBINATION OF BOTH.

NO-EGG OATMEAL-NUT COOKIES [X]

3/4 CUP LIGHT BROWN SUGAR, FIRMLY PACKED

1 1/2 STICKS SOFT BUTTER

2 TEASPOONS VANILLA

1 1/2 CUPS QUICK-COOKING OATS

1 CUP FLOUR

1/2 TEASPOON BAKING SODA

1/2 CUP CHOPPED NUTS

1. IN LARGE MIXING BOWL CREAM BUTTER AND SUGAR UNTIL LIGHT AND FLUFFY. ADD VANILLA.

2. COMBINE DRY INGREDIENTS AND ADD TO CREAMED MIXTURE.

3. CHILL FOR 20 MINUTES. FORM DOUGH INTO 4 ROLLS 1 INCH IN DIAMETER.

4. SET OVEN TO 375°F. CUT IN 1/2-INCH PIECES AND ROLL EACH PIECE INTO A BALL. PLACE ON UNGREASED COOKIE SHEET. (COOKIE SHEETS HOLD APPROXIMATELY 15 COOKIES EACH.) DIP THE BOTTOM OF A SMALL GLASS INTO FLOUR AND FLATTEN COOKIES. REFLOUR GLASS AS NEEDED.

5. BAKE FOR ABOUT 12 MINUTES OR UNTIL GOLDEN BROWN. THIS RECIPE MAKES CRISP OATMEAL-NUT COOKIES 2 INCHES IN DIAMETER.

YIELD: APPROXIMATELY 5 DOZEN COOKIES

VARIATIONS:

FOR OATMEAL CHOCOLATE CHIP COOKIES ADD 3/4 CUP CHOCOLATE CHIPS TO ABOVE OR FOR OATMEAL RAISIN COOKIES, OMIT NUTS AND ADD 3/4 CUP RAISINS.

COCONUT OATMEAL COOKIES [X]

1 CUP SIFTED FLOUR
1/2 TEASPOON BAKING POWDER
1/2 TEASPOON BAKING SODA
1/2 TEASPOON SALT
1/2 CUP BUTTER

1/2 CUP GRANULATED SUGAR
1/2 CUP BROWN SUGAR
1 EGG
1 TEASPOON VANILLA
1/2 CUP QUICK-COOKING OATS

1/2 CUP FLAKED COCONUT AND ADDITIONAL COCONUT

1. SIFT FLOUR WITH BAKING POWDER, BAKING SODA, AND SALT.

2. CREAM BUTTER. GRADUALLY ADD SUGARS. CREAM UNTIL LIGHT AND FLUFFY. ADD EGG AND VANILLA. BEAT WELL.

3. ADD FLOUR MIXTURE IN ABOUT 4 EQUAL PARTS, BEATING UNTIL JUST SMOOTH AFTER EACH ADDITION. MIX IN OATS AND COCONUT. COVER AND CHILL DOUGH FOR 1 HOUR. SET OVEN TO 375°F APPROXIMATELY 10 MINUTES BEFORE BAKING.

4. PUT ADDITIONAL COCONUT IN PLASTIC BAG. FORM CHILLED DOUGH INTO 4 ROLLS, APPROXIMATELY 1 INCH IN DIAMETER. CUT INTO 1-INCH PIECES AND ROLL INTO BALLS. PUT 3 BALLS IN BAG AND SHAKE LIGHTLY. PLACE 3 ACROSS ON UNGREASED COOKIE SHEET. COOKIES WILL SPREAD DURING BAKING. BAKE FOR 9 TO 12 MINUTES, OR UNTIL GOLDEN BROWN. FOR EASIER REMOVAL, LEAVE COOKIES ON TRAY FOR ABOUT 5 MINUTES.

YIELD: APPROXIMATELY 4 DOZEN

APRICOT SQUARES [F]

---

1 1/2 CUPS FLOUR

1 TEASPOON BAKING POWDER

1/4 TEASPOON SALT

1 1/2 CUPS QUICK-COOKING OATS

1 CUP BROWN SUGAR

3/4 CUP COLD BUTTER

1 CUP APRICOT JAM

1. SET OVEN TO 350°F.

2. MIX FLOUR, BAKING POWDER, SALT, OATS, AND SUGAR. CUT BUTTER IN CHUNKS. IN FOOD PROCESSOR, WHIRL ABOVE INGREDIENTS WITH BUTTER FOR A FEW SECONDS OR UNTIL MIXTURE RESEMBLES COARSE CORNMEAL.

3. PAT TWO-THIRDS OF THE CRUMB MIXTURE INTO A 7 X 11-INCH PAN. SPREAD WITH JAM. COVER WITH REMAINING CRUMB MIXTURE. BAKE FOR ABOUT 30 TO 35 MINUTES OR UNTIL BROWNED. COOL. CUT INTO 1 1/2-INCH SQUARES.

YIELD: APPROXIMATELY 3 DOZEN SQUARES

WHEN WE WERE TRAVELING IN VERMONT, WE DISCOVERED THIS SAME RECIPE MADE WITH SEEDLESS RASPBERRY JAM, SLIGHTLY WARMED. IT WAS TRULY DELICIOUS!

CHOCOLATE BUTTONS [M, X]

6 TABLESPOONS VEGETABLE OIL
4 SQUARES UNSWEETENED CHOCOLATE
2 CUPS SUGAR
4 EGGS
2 TEASPOONS VANILLA

2 CUPS FLOUR
2 TEASPOONS BAKING POWDER
1/2 TEASPOON SALT
3/4 CUP CHOPPED NUTS
1 CUP CONFECTIONERS' SUGAR

1. MELT CHOCOLATE IN MICROWAVE OVEN. SET ASIDE TO COOL.

2. IN LARGE MIXER BOWL, COMBINE VEGETABLE OIL, MELTED CHOCOLATE, AND SUGAR. BEAT IN EGGS, 1 AT A TIME. ADD VANILLA.

3. SIFT FLOUR, BAKING POWDER, AND SALT TOGETHER. BLEND INTO CHOCOLATE MIXTURE. ADD NUTS AND MIX. COVER AND REFRIGERATE A FEW HOURS OR OVERNIGHT.

4. AN HOUR BEFORE BAKING, REMOVE DOUGH FROM REFRIGERATOR. SET OVEN TO 350°F. GREASE COOKIE SHEETS.

5. PLACE CONFECTIONERS' SUGAR IN A SMALL PLASTIC BAG. FORM COOKIE DOUGH INTO 4 ROLLS ABOUT 1 INCH IN DIAMETER. CUT ROLLS INTO 1/4- TO 1/2-INCH SLICES. ROLL INTO BALLS THE SIZE OF WALNUTS OR SMALLER. PLACE 4 COOKIE DOUGH BALLS AT A TIME INTO BAG OF CONFECTIONERS' SUGAR. SHAKE BAG. REMOVE BALLS FROM BAG AND SHAKE OFF EXCESS SUGAR.

6. PUT 4 ACROSS ON COOKIE SHEET ABOUT 1 1/2 TO 2 INCHES APART IN FIVE ROWS. BAKE FOR 10 TO 13 MINUTES. COOKIES WILL BE MOIST.

YIELD: APPROXIMATELY 8 DOZEN COOKIES

CHOCOLATE CORDIAL CONFECTIONS [M]

1 CUP CHOCOLATE CHIPS   3 TABLESPOONS LIGHT CORN SYRUP
1/2 CUP CORDIAL OF YOUR CHOICE
2 1/2 CUPS CRUSHED VANILLA WAFERS
1/2 CUP AND ADDITIONAL CONFECTIONERS' SUGAR FOR ROLLING
1 CUP MEDIUM CHOPPED PECANS OR WALNUTS

1. MELT CHOCOLATE CHIPS IN MICROWAVE. ADD CORN SYRUP
   AND CORDIAL.

2. COMBINE VANILLA WAFERS, CONFECTIONERS' SUGAR, AND NUTS TO
   OTHER INGREDIENTS AND BLEND WELL.

3. REFRIGERATE FOR 20 MINUTES.

4. FORM INTO 4 ROLLS 1 INCH IN DIAMETER. SLICE INTO 1/2-INCH
   PIECES. ROLL EACH PIECE INTO A BALL.

5. PLACE CONFECTIONERS' SUGAR IN A SMALL PLASTIC BAG. PLACE
   4 BALLS AT A TIME INTO BAG AND SHAKE. REMOVE BALLS FROM
   BAG AND SERVE OR STORE.

YIELD: 9 DOZEN SPHERES

*STORE IN TIGHTLY COVERED CONTAINER. CAN BE FROZEN. PLACED IN
DECORATIVE TINS, THESE MAKE MARVELOUS HOLIDAY GIFTS.*

CREAM CHEESE FROSTING [X]

6 OUNCES CREAM CHEESE
2 TABLESPOONS BUTTER

2 CUPS POWDERED SUGAR, SIFTED
2 TEASPOONS VANILLA

1. SOFTEN CREAM CHEESE AND BUTTER AND COMBINE IN MIXING BOWL.

2. ADD POWDERED SUGAR AND VANILLA. BEAT UNTIL SMOOTH.

YIELD: ABOUT 2 CUPS

JAN'S CHOCOLATE LOVER'S FROSTING [M, X]

4 SQUARES UNSWEETENED CHOCOLATE
3 CUPS CONFECTIONERS' SUGAR

1/2 CUP EVAPORATED MILK
1/3 CUP SOFTENED BUTTER

1. MELT CHOCOLATE IN MICROWAVE OVEN. SET ASIDE TO COOL.

2. COMBINE CONFECTIONERS' SUGAR WITH EVAPORATED MILK.

3. ADD COOLED CHOCOLATE AND MIX WELL. STIR IN SOFTENED BUTTER. BEAT UNTIL LIGHT AND FLUFFY. REFRIGERATE SLIGHTLY IF TOO THIN.

YIELD: APPROXIMATELY 2 CUPS

DOUBLE NUT TOPPING [M]

1/2 CUP PACKED BROWN SUGAR	1/4 CUP BUTTER

2 TABLESPOONS FROZEN ORANGE JUICE CONCENTRATE, THAWED

1 CUP FLAKED COCONUT	1/2 CUP CHOPPED WALNUTS

1. COMBINE BROWN SUGAR, BUTTER, AND ORANGE JUICE CONCENTRATE IN SMALL SAUCEPAN. BRING TO BOILING ON STOVETOP OR IN MICROWAVE. COOK 1 MINUTE, STIRRING FREQUENTLY.

2. ADD COCONUT AND WALNUTS.

YIELD: APPROXIMATELY 1 1/2 CUPS

BROILED COCONUT FROSTING

2 TABLESPOONS BUTTER	1/4 CUP EVAPORATED MILK
3/4 CUP DARK BROWN SUGAR	1 CUP FLAKED COCONUT

COMBINE ALL INGREDIENTS. SPREAD OVER COOLED CAKE. BROIL UNDER PREHEATED BROILER UNTIL BROWN AND BUBBLY.

YIELD: ENOUGH FROSTING FOR A 9 X 13-INCH CAKE

ODDS & ENDS

ODDS & ENDS

HINTS:

FOR YOUR INFORMATION, HERE IS A LIST OF PERCENTAGE OF CALORIES FROM FAT FOR COMMON NUTS AND SEEDS, TAKEN FROM A USDA BOOK, *COMPOSITION OF FOODS*.

TYPE	%	TYPE	%
ALMONDS, DRIED	54.2	PINE, PIGNOLIA	47.4
ALMONDS, ROASTED	57.7	PINE, PIÑON	60.5
BRAZILS	66.9	PISTACHIOS	53.7
CASHEWS	45.7	PUMPKIN SEEDS	46.7
FILBERTS (HAZELNUTS)	62.4	SUNFLOWER SEEDS	47.3
PEANUTS, ROASTED	26.0	WALNUTS, BLACK	59.3
PECANS	71.2	WALNUTS, ENGLISH	64.0

APPLE CHUTNEY [F, M]

2 CUPS GRATED OR CHOPPED APPLES
1 TEASPOON LEMON JUICE
1/2 CUP RAISINS
3/4 CUP MOLASSES

1/2 CUP CIDER VINEGAR
1/2 TEASPOON SALT
1 TEASPOON GINGER
1 TEASPOON DRY MUSTARD

1 TABLESPOON CURRY POWDER OR TO TASTE

1. MIX INGREDIENTS TOGETHER. BRING TO A BOIL ON STOVE, STIRRING CONSTANTLY. SIMMER UNCOVERED ON LOW HEAT FOR 15 MINUTES, STIRRING OFTEN.

OR

IF USING MICROWAVE, BRING TO A BOIL. STIR AND REDUCE TO 50% POWER. SIMMER FOR 15 MINUTES, STIRRING EVERY MINUTE.

2. COOL. PLACE IN COVERED CONTAINER. REFRIGERATE.

YIELD: 3 CUPS

USE THIS AS AN ACCOMPANIMENT TO **INDIAN CURRIED CHICKEN**.

"YOUR OWN" DRY-ROASTED NUTS

1 POUND RAW NUTS   SALT AND/OR OTHER SEASONING

1. SET OVEN TO 350°F. PLACE NUTS OF YOUR CHOICE IN A SINGLE LAYER IN A JELLY ROLL PAN (10 1/2 X 15 1/2 INCHES). POUR PLAIN TAP WATER OVER NUTS AND PAT THEM DOWN WITH YOUR FINGERS SO THAT THEY ARE ENTIRELY COVERED BY WATER. ALLOW TO STAND AT ROOM TEMPERATURE FOR 15 MINUTES.

2. DRAIN THE NUTS IN A LARGE COLANDER. DO NOT RINSE, BUT SHAKE THE COLANDER A BIT TO REMOVE EXCESS MOISTURE. SHAKE SALT OVER DAMP PAN SURFACE.

3. RETURN NUTS TO PAN AND SPREAD SO NUTS ARE IN A SINGLE LAYER. SHAKE MORE SALT OVER THE TOP OF NUTS. IF A SALTY/SWEET FLAVOR IS DESIRED, COAT PAN WITH SALT AND THEN SUGAR. PLACE NUTS ON PAN. SPRINKLE WITH SUGAR AND THEN SALT.

4. PLACE IN OVEN AND BAKE APPROXIMATELY 30 MINUTES. STIR WITH A WOODEN UTENSIL EVERY 10 MINUTES, MAKING SURE TO REARRANGE NUTS FROM CORNERS AND EDGES INTO CENTER. BAKING TIME WILL DEPEND ON SIZE OF NUTS AND DEGREE OF TOASTING DESIRED. THE NUTS WILL CONTINUE TO DRY AS THEY COOL.

5. STIR AGAIN AFTER REMOVING PAN FROM OVEN. COOL COMPLETELY.

6. PACKAGE IN HEAVY PLASTIC BAG OR OTHER AIRTIGHT CONTAINER. THE FLAVOR IS BETTER DEVELOPED AFTER 24 HOURS.

YIELD: 1 POUND DRY-ROASTED NUTS

PEACHY SPICED PEACHES

1 LARGE CAN PEACH HALVES   1 TEASPOON WHOLE ALLSPICE
1 TEASPOON WHOLE CLOVES   1/2 CUP BROWN SUGAR
1/2 CUP VINEGAR

1. DRAIN PEACH HALVES, SAVING SYRUP. SET PEACHES ASIDE.

2. IN A LARGE SAUCEPAN, COMBINE SYRUP, CLOVES, ALLSPICE, BROWN SUGAR, AND VINEGAR. BOIL UNTIL SUGAR IS DISSOLVED.

3. ADD PEACHES AND SIMMER ABOUT 8 MINUTES. COOL IN SYRUP.

YIELD: APPROXIMATELY 6 TO 8 SERVINGS

THESE PEACHES ARE A NICE ACCOMPANIMENT TO HAM OR PORK CHOPS. SAME RECIPE MAY ALSO BE USED FOR CANNED PEARS.

FEELING YOUR OATS GRANOLA

4 CUPS ROLLED OATS	1/2 CUP COCONUT
1 CUP WHEAT GERM	1/3 CUP OIL*
1 CUP CHOPPED NUTS	1/3 CUP HONEY

1 1/2 CUPS DICED, DRIED FRUIT OF YOUR CHOICE**

1. SET OVEN TO 300°F. MIX ROLLED OATS, WHEAT GERM, NUTS, AND COCONUT TOGETHER.

2. COMBINE OIL AND HONEY AND ADD TO THE ABOVE. STIR WELL.

3. SPREAD ON A COOKIE SHEET. BAKE FOR 15 MINUTES, STIRRING FREQUENTLY.

4. ADD 1 CUP DICED, DRIED FRUIT. STORE IN CLOSED CONTAINER.

YIELD: 8 CUPS

*WE RECOMMEND CANOLA OIL AS IT IS BLAND IN FLAVOR AND LOW IN SATURATED FAT.

**BE IMAGINATIVE—TRY ANY OR ALL OF THE FOLLOWING DRIED FRUITS: RAISINS, APRICOTS, BANANAS, APPLES, PEACHES, PAPAYA, AND PINEAPPLE. WE MADE A HAWAIIAN MIX USING DRIED PINEAPPLE, PAPAYA, BANANA, AND MACADAMIA NUTS.

PEANUT BRITTLE [M]

1 CUP SUGAR	1 CUP SHELLED ROASTED PEANUTS*
1/2 CUP LIGHT CORN SYRUP	1 TABLESPOON BUTTER
DASH OF SALT	1 1/2 TEASPOONS VANILLA
	1 TEASPOON BAKING SODA

1. GREASE BAKING SHEET **HEAVILY.** SET OVEN TO 300°F.

2. COMBINE SUGAR, CORN SYRUP, AND SALT IN 2-QUART MICROWAVE-SAFE BOWL. MICROWAVE ON HIGH FOR 4 MINUTES, STIRRING ONCE OR TWICE. PUT BAKING SHEET IN OVEN. ADD PEANUTS TO SUGAR MIXTURE AND RETURN TO MICROWAVE. MICROWAVE ON HIGH FOR 4 MINUTES, STIRRING ONCE OR TWICE.

3. STIR BUTTER AND VANILLA INTO SUGAR MIXTURE. ADD BAKING SODA **LAST.** STIR AGAIN. MIXTURE WILL BE FOAMY.

4. REMOVE BAKING SHEET FROM OVEN. QUICKLY AND CAREFULLY SPREAD PEANUT BRITTLE ON **HOT** BAKING SHEET USING A METAL SPOON. SPREAD AS THIN AS POSSIBLE.

5. COOL AND BREAK INTO PIECES.

YIELD: 1 POUND

PECANS, CASHEWS, OR ANY NUT OF YOUR CHOICE MAY BE USED IN PLACE OF PEANUTS.

THIS RECIPE IS INTENDED FOR USE WITH 900-WATT MICROWAVE OVENS. TIMING IN OTHER SIZE OVENS WILL VARY.

TREATS FOR YOUR CANINE FRIENDS [F]

2 1/2 CUPS WHOLE WHEAT FLOUR

1 TEASPOON BROWN SUGAR

1/2 CUP POWDERED MILK

1 BOUILLON CUBE

1/2 CUP PEANUT BUTTER OR GRATED CHEESE

6 TABLESPOONS BUTTER

1 BEATEN EGG

2/3 CUP COLD WATER

1. SET OVEN TO 225°F.

2. COMBINE FLOUR, POWDERED MILK, BROWN SUGAR, AND BOULLION CUBE IN A FOOD PROCESSOR FOR A FEW SECONDS. ADD PEANUT BUTTER OR CHEESE AND BUTTER.

3. MIX EGG WITH WATER AND ADD SLOWLY TO INGREDIENTS IN FOOD PROCESSOR. PROCESS UNTIL DOUGH HOLDS TOGETHER.

4. ROLL ONTO FLOURED BOARD, CUT WITH A PIZZA CUTTER INTO DOGGIE-SIZED BITES AND BAKE FOR ABOUT 2 TO 3 HOURS, OR UNTIL BISCUITS ARE HARD. BISCUITS CAN BE LEFT IN THE OVEN OVERNIGHT WITH THE OVEN TURNED OFF TO THOROUGHLY DRY THEM OUT AND MAKE THEM CRUNCHY. THE NUMBER OF BISCUITS THIS RECIPE MAKES DEPENDS ON THE SIZE YOUR DOG LIKES.

OUR CANINE FRIEND PREFERS THE CHEESE VARIETY.

INDEX

EASY ELEGANT DINING INDEX

EASY ELEGANT DINING **INDEX** (CONTINUED)

EASY ELEGANT DINING INDEX (CONTINUED)

EASY ELEGANT DINING INDEX (CONTINUED)

EASY ELEGANT DINING **INDEX** (CONTINUED)

EASY ELEGANT DINING INDEX (CONTINUED)

EASY ELEGANT DINING INDEX (CONTINUED)

WHAT OTHERS ARE SAYING ABOUT
EASY ELEGANT DINING:

---

*"AN OCCUPATIONAL THERAPIST'S AIM IS TO SEE EVERY INDIVIDUAL REACH HIS OR HER HIGHEST POTENTIAL FOR INDEPENDENT, PRODUCTIVE LIVING. **EASY ELEGANT DINING** IS VALUABLE TO HANDICAPPED PEOPLE WHO WISH TO ENTERTAIN AT DINNER WITH EASE AND ELEGANCE."*

HOPE E. GESSNER, CERTIFIED OCCUPATIONAL THERAPY ASSISTANT, LICENSED

*"WHAT A TREAT! I CAN READ **EASY ELEGANT DINING** WITHOUT MY GLASSES. THE FREQUENT AND CREATIVE USE OF MODERN KITCHEN APPLIANCES MAKES THE PREPARATION OF THESE RECIPES EASY."*

JUDITH M. HARTZELL, HUMAN SERVICES COORDINATOR AND COUNSELOR

*"**EASY ELEGANT DINING** IS A DELIGHT. IT TAKES CLASSIC MENU ITEMS THAT ARE PRACTICAL AND HAVE GREAT APPEAL INTO THE REALITY OF TODAY'S BUSY AND COMPLEX WORLD."*

RICHARD A. BENEFIELD, RETIRED GENERAL MANAGER, THE NITTANY LION INN, PENNSYLVANIA STATE UNIVERSITY

*"AS A CAREER WOMAN AND MOTHER OF AN ACTIVE DAUGHTER, I HAVE FOUND THAT **EASY ELEGANT DINING** IS FILLED WITH INTERESTING RECIPES THAT ARE BOTH EASY TO CREATE, YET ELEGANT TO SERVE."*

JANET L. WEINHOFER, DIRECTOR OF HUMAN RESOURCES

REDISCOVER THE FUN AND SATISFACTION OF COOKING
ORDER *EASY ELEGANT DINING* NOW!

YES! ENCLOSED IS MY ORDER. *EASY ELEGANT DINING* IS $19.95 PLUS $4.00 S/H EACH (TOTAL $23.95 PER BOOK). PLEASE SEND ME _____ COPIES OF *EASY ELEGANT DINING*.

BOOK(S) AND SHIPPING TOTAL $ _____

PA ADDRESS ADD 6% SALES TAX $ _____

TOTAL $ _____

YOUR NAME _____

STREET _____ APT. _____

CITY, STATE _____ ZIP _____

TELEPHONE NUMBER _____

METHOD OF PAYMENT: ☐ CHECK ☐ VISA ☐ MASTERCARD

CREDIT CARD # _____ EXP. DATE _____

SIGNATURE _____

PLEASE USE REVERSE SIDE FOR GIFT ORDERS.

MAKE CHECKS PAYABLE TO TIA PUBLISHING, P. O. BOX 567, EMMAUS, PA 18049-0567

FOR FASTER SERVICE OR FOR ORDERS OF THREE OR MORE BOOKS, CALL (800) 772-5069, (215) 967-3607, OR FAX (215) 965-4360.

THANK YOU FOR YOUR ORDER!

GIFT ORDERS FOR
EASY ELEGANT DINING

WOULD YOU LIKE US TO INCLUDE A GIFT CARD IN YOUR NAME?
PLEASE MAKE AN "X" IN THE BOX FOR GIFT ORDERS.

NAME _____ ☐

STREET _____ APT. _____

CITY, STATE _____ ZIP _____

SIGN GIFT CARD _____

NAME _____ ☐

STREET _____ APT. _____

CITY, STATE _____ ZIP _____

SIGN GIFT CARD _____

NAME _____ ☐

STREET _____ APT. _____

CITY, STATE _____ ZIP _____

SIGN GIFT CARD _____

NAME _____ ☐

STREET _____ APT. _____

CITY, STATE _____ ZIP _____

SIGN GIFT CARD _____